LEGISLATION AND SERVICES FOR
CHILDREN AND YOUNG PEOPLE IN NORTHERN IRELAND

Report of the Children
and Young Persons
Review Group

DECEMBER 1979

BELFAST
HER MAJESTY'S STATIONERY OFFICE

LEGISLATION AND SERVICES FOR
CHILDREN AND YOUNG PERSONS IN NORTHERN IRELAND

Report of the Children and Young Persons Review Group

DECEMBER 1979

BELFAST
HER MAJESTY'S STATIONERY OFFICE
£2.25 net

Children and Young Persons
Review Group

Membership

SIR HAROLD BLACK   *Chairman*

F. A. ELLIOTT (To October 1976)
J. A. WILDE   *Department of Health and*
R. F. MILLS   *Social Services*
Dr. M. N. HAYES (From October 1976)

J. H. PARKES (To January 1977)
R. S. STERLING (To October 1977)
S. H. JAMIESON (From January 1977)
J. J. O. MCCLENAHAN (From October 1977) *Northern Ireland Office*
J. B. BOURN (To October 1977)
J. A. MARSHALL (From October 1977)

P. J. GRANT (From February 1976)   *Office of the Legislative*
                                    Draftsmen
R. T. HOLMES (From January 1978)   *Department of Education*

Joint Secretaries
W. J. KIRKPATRICK
R. WILSON (To June 1979)
Miss J. A. MILLS (From February 1979)

Foreword

In the course of our work we have been much impressed by the dedication of the many people in both statutory and voluntary sectors who are involved with children and young people. This has been evident in the visits we have undertaken in Northern Ireland and in the discussions on the Consultative Document. In preparing the Report which we now submit we have been greatly assisted by the information and views presented to us in written and oral evidence and we wish to thank all those who contributed.

We are indebted to our secretaries and to Mr. J. L. Townson and Mrs. M. F. M. Hunter who assisted in arranging meetings, taking minutes, preparing papers and recording the oral evidence. Particular thanks are due to Mr. R. Wilson for his painstaking consideration of the available literature and for his skilful presentation of the relevant material. We wish also to thank Mr. J. Harbison and Dr. Jean Graham of the Social Research Division, Central Economic Service for research carried out on our behalf.

Contents

I— Introduction

To: Michael Alison Esq., MP, Minister of State.

Lord Elton, Parliamentary Under Secretary of State.

1.1 We were appointed in January 1976 by the then Minister of State for Health and Social Services, Mr. Roland Moyle MP, and Lord Donaldson, Parliamentary Under Secretary at the Northern Ireland Office. Our terms of reference were:—

(a) to review legislation and services relating to the care and treatment of children and young persons under the Children and Young Persons Act (Northern Ireland) 1968, the Adoption Act (Northern Ireland) 1967 and the Probation Act (Northern Ireland) 1950 taking into account developments in these fields in Great Britain;

(b) to consider in particular the future administration of the Northern Ireland Probation Service; and

(c) to make recommendations as to changes in legislation and organisation in these services in Northern Ireland.

1.2 The first meeting was held on 12 January 1976 and in all there were 24 meetings. In addition, members of the Group have visited a number of children's homes and training schools for juveniles in Northern Ireland together with other facilities for young people in need or in trouble, and have also taken the opportunity to observe how proceedings are conducted in juvenile courts in Northern Ireland.

1.3 Our deliberations have taken account of Government and Parliamentary Reports and comment from a wide variety of sources, including practitioners and academics, on the services for children[1] in the rest of the United Kingdom. We considered unpublished local research "Community Support Survey 1977" and "Children in Care in Northern Ireland" carried out by the Social Research Division of the Central Economic Service. We have also been in close touch with developments in England, and members of the Group have visited Scotland to observe the operation of the system there, and individual visits have been paid also to the United States, Holland and Western Germany. Other systems throughout the world have been considered, including those in Scandinavia, Canada and the Republic of Ireland.

1.4 Taking the provisions of the Children and Young Persons Act (Northern Ireland) 1968 as the basis for discussion, we issued a consultative document in June 1977 which dealt with all our terms of reference except adoption which has been considered separately. Following the issue of that document we received written evidence from a large number of organisations and individuals and subsequently heard oral evidence. This evidence, being based on a wealth of knowledge and experience, was of great value and we have drawn heavily upon it. A list of the organisations and individuals who submitted written and oral evidence is contained in the Appendix.

---

1. Throughout the Report we use the term "child" to cover children and young persons in the age range 0–17 years. Similarly for convenience we refer to both boys and girls as "he".

1.5 Although our terms of reference included the examination of policy and legislation relating to adoption, we considered that these issues merited a separate exercise and, accordingly, a sub-group was established for this purpose in March 1977. On the basis of the sub-group's work, a consultative paper was recently prepared. Final recommendations will be the subject of a separate report.

1.6 We appreciate that the recommendations included in this Report, if accepted by Ministers, could have far-reaching implications and we emphasise the need to have adequate resources to meet the proposed changes. The 1969 Act in England and Wales has been severely criticised but its proponents continue to argue that its proper implementation can never be achieved unless adequate resources are made available. The question of resources is raised again later in the Report[2].

---

2. Paragraph 8.5 et seq.

2— Background

2.1 There is temptation in a review of this nature to give so much attention to controversial or popular issues that other matters are overlooked or given cursory and superficial treatment. For example, it was obvious that a view would have to be taken on the welfare versus justice debate which has been so divisive elsewhere in the United Kingdom and which seemed, from the evidence presented to us, to be no less divisive here. However, to our mind this is a secondary issue; the primary determinant of children's behaviour in Northern Ireland, or anywhere else for that matter, is the social, moral and economic climate within which they have to grow up.

2.2 Evidence accumulated over the last decade demonstrates that the social and environmental disadvantages experienced by children in their earliest years can influence their intellectual, social and emotional development. The problem in Northern Ireland is, therefore, formidable. There can be no room for complacency when so many children are faced with what amounts to multiple deprivation arising from poverty, poor living conditions, long-term unemployment, and a poor social and physical environment. On top of this and the rapidly changing nature of modern society there is also the continuing problem of political and social instability associated with the decade of civil unrest. We concentrate first of all, therefore, on the social and economic background against which the child care agencies have to work.

2.3 Levels of income in Northern Ireland are the lowest of any region in the United Kingdom. High unemployment, a lower average wage, a significantly higher birth rate, larger families and a higher dependancy ratio (the proportion of economically inactive people in the population, including children and the elderly) all contribute to the relative poverty of the area. In Northern Ireland nearly twice as many households with children have low incomes as in the United Kingdom as a whole (35% as against 18% in 1976).[3]

2.4 Unemployment is a chronic problem central to many social ills in the Province. In the post-war period the annual level of unemployment in Northern Ireland has consistently been above that of all other regions in the United Kingdom. During the 1960's, for example, the level of unemployment was generally three times that of the whole of the United Kingdom and about double the rate for Scotland and Wales. The situation for young people is equally serious. The number of unemployed young people (under 19) has been growing steadily during the 1970's. In March 1979 (before either of the two summer school-leaving dates) over 2,200 school-leavers were without work, approximately twice the level in England. At the same date almost 7,000 young people under 19 were unemployed.

2.5 A survey of the housing stock of Northern Ireland, made in 1974 by the Northern Ireland Housing Executive, showed that half of the houses in Northern Ireland were built before 1945 and a third before 1920. Only 16.5% of the housing stock belongs to the inter-war period, when there was a massive housing renewal in parts of Britain. As a result, some 20% of dwellings in use

---

3. Economic and Social Progress in Northern Ireland. Review and Prospects. 1978. HMSO.

are classed as statutorily unfit, and a further 17.5% need substantial improvements to bring them up to modern standards. Of the unfit dwellings in urban areas many are in the Belfast inner city.

2.6 Urban renewal has brought its own problems. Delay in completing urban renewal plans (only 4,000 dwellings were built in Belfast between October 1973 and December 1978) has been accompanied by movement of people out of Belfast. Migration from the inner city has also increased the demand for housing outside the city and in nearby towns. There, housing conditions, particularly in the new estates, are usually very much better than in the inner city. Available housing has not, however, always matched family size and in some estates there is serious overcrowding. Vandalism and destruction have become features of some of the new housing estates, particularly those with a high ratio of children and an absence of facilities which provide the foundation for the growth of communities—playgrounds, community social centres, shops, schools, health clinics. In the last few years significant strides have been taken to provide adequate facilities. This must be accompanied by widespread encouragement of children to make use of these provisions and to respect them. Parents too have a part to play in encouraging a more responsible attitude in their children and respect for community facilities and the property of others.

2.7 Whilst there have been impressive advances in education in Northern Ireland over the past 10–15 years such as the modernisation of buildings, the reduction of class sizes and the development of the home/school links programme, a number of problems remain. There is, for example, an unacceptably high level of persistent non-attendance at school: in one term in 1977 over 14,000 children of compulsory school age were absent for over 25% of the term without justifiable reason. Evidence suggests that the problem is at its worst among older children (age 15 and 16) and in the main urban centres of Belfast and Londonderry. Nine schools containing 3% of the school population accounted for over 13% of extreme non-attenders (missing half or more of the term).

2.8 The lack of provision for the under fives was clearly illustrated in a recent policy document[4] which showed that provision in Northern Ireland for the under fives, whether in nursery education or in other pre-school provision, falls far short of that available in England and Wales. In 1977 only 6.5% of 3 and 4 year-olds in Northern Ireland attended nursery schools compared to 10.2% in England and Wales: similarly the rate of provision of places in pre-school playgroups was only about 50% of that in England and Wales. Even though a greater proportion of 4 year-olds in Northern Ireland are enrolled in primary schools than is the case in England and Wales, the fact is that the lack of more extensive provision for young children in Northern Ireland bears particularly on those already subject to the stress of bad housing and low incomes. We touch on this problem specifically later in the Report[5].

2.9 In considering the problems that children face in Northern Ireland our discussions must inevitably take into account the effects of ten years of civil unrest. The effects of this conflict on society are difficult to assess. This was apparent from the evidence we received which, whilst acknowledging the civil

4. Day Care and Education for the Under Fives in Northern Ireland, Department of Health and Social Services and Department of Education. 1978.
5. Paragraph 3.27.

4

unrest as a factor which could not be ignored, invariably was not specific on the impact it might have on the issues under review.

2.10 To some extent the consequences of the past decade are there for all to see. The growth of paramilitary organisations gave rise to organised terrorism and intimidation, and brutalised many young people who have come under their influence. The facts and figures of those killed and injured and the extent of damage to property are an indictment in themselves but does the harm not go even deeper? Communities have been driven into isolation; social and economic life has been disrupted; the influence of traditional leaders has been eroded, as has the authority of the State; the level of violence has been raised as has the threshold of tolerance. Thus children are being raised in a community where many of the norms which form the framework for society have been removed without any adequate replacement, and many of the landmarks which provide direction and stability for the growing child have been destroyed or obscured.

2.11 When so many children are being brought up under adverse social and economic conditions, compounded by civil unrest, it might be expected that the statistics of juvenile delinquency would indicate a higher rate than in the rest of the United Kingdom. In fact the figures for juveniles convicted of indictable offences per 100,000 population are lower than in England and Wales, and indeed have fallen since the beginning of civil unrest in 1969. However, the conviction rate is not a wholly satisfactory measure of delinquency: the detection rate and the fact that the police have been occupied with serious terrorist crime must be taken into account. The figures should therefore be viewed with caution. In fact it is probable that juvenile crime in Northern Ireland has increased during the last ten years. A particularly disturbing feature is the increase in crimes of violence against the person by juveniles.

2.12 If the depressed economic situation in Northern Ireland and the poor physical environment in which many children live are factors which can contribute to the incidence of juvenile crime, then there may be other forces within Northern Ireland's society which provide at least a partial counter-balance. In Northern Ireland, the family and particularly the extended family has always been a strong force within society. It has been suggested to us that the influence of family upon individuals is weakening but that the extended family in Northern Ireland is still a relatively strong influence. In support of this argument it is also pointed out that, in spite of the economic and environmental problems, the number of children taken into care in Northern Ireland is only 60% of the rate in England and Wales. The churches are another significant influence within Northern Ireland's society and in many areas there is still a recognisable sense of community, which in some ways has been heightened as the tensions of the last ten years have isolated small communities and forced them to become more introverted.

2.13 A caring community must concern itself with the quality of life it offers to all its children. We take the view that the resources of the community must be directed to helping not only children in trouble but children in need and our first priority, therefore, is to stress the need for a comprehensive strategy of help for such children. Our ideas on this are set out more fully in the next chapter.

3—A Strategy for Help

3.1 Our concern in the previous chapter, in highlighting some of the fundamental problems facing Government and society, was to place our own recommendations in perspective. These recommendations cannot be a panacea for the needs of children. We hope, however, that what we suggest will go some way towards rationalising and improving upon existing arrangements for identifying and helping those children who, without such help, are likely to attract some form of compulsory intervention either because of educational needs, social or family problems or because they get into trouble with the police.

3.2 The needs of children are many and varied. In some cases the need is all too apparent—a child subjected to physical abuse clearly needs protection. In other cases a lack of attainment at school, apathy, persistent misbehaviour, truancy, or involvement in delinquent or criminal activity may be the outward manifestation of complex personal or family problems. In our view there is an onus on society to take account as early as possible of these and other problems faced by children in growing up. We do not have any illusions that this can be achieved other than by a whole-hearted effort on the part of parents, local communities, voluntary organisations and the various social, educational and youth services working together to this end.

3.3 The approach which we recommend lays emphasis on prevention. Where problems do occur, early and accurate identification of the specific difficulties is desirable followed by co-ordinated, flexible and effective action. We advocate a comprehensive and integrated approach to the provision of help and support for children whose personality, background or circumstances leave them ill-equipped to cope with the demands and pressures of society. The provision of help should be the responsibility of the normal social and educational services. While the aim should be to create a climate in which potential users will voluntarily seek the support of these agencies in resolving their problems, there must be some formal framework through which the various agencies can come together to review and co-ordinate their joint activities. In advocating machinery for co-ordination, however, we are conscious that help for children in need can most appropriately and effectively be provided within a family setting. But the family may need support and must be able to look for this to the wider community, which has a direct responsibility for the future of its children.

HELP THROUGH THE FAMILY

3.4 The family is the first and most basic institution in our society for developing a child's potential. Other influences do not enter a child's life until after the first few, formative, years. It is within the family that the child experiences love, attention, care, supervision, discipline, conflict, neglect, stress or abuse depending on parental and family characteristics and circumstances. It is within the family that the child learns about the management of emotion and the development of responsiveness to others. Inadequate parental guidance, changing parental figures, and lack of parental competence can inhibit the overall development of children.

6

3.5 We consider that society must seek to develop and provide the environment, resources and opportunities through which families can become more competent to deal with their own problems. Better housing, better recreational facilities, increased employment opportunities, adequate family income, education in family planning will all help to create a supportive framework within which the relationships of the family can develop. Adult figures provide the standards of behaviour and children are likely to model themselves on those with whom they have had close relationships. For many couples, however, no formal preparation for marriage and parenthood is available and poor parenting practices can be perpetuated in future generations through the process of imitation. We consider that this might be counteracted by the provision of education for parenthood as part of a co-ordinated service to be provided not only by schools but also through Health and Social Services Board staff and voluntary agencies. We endorse the views on education for parenthood set out in the White Paper "Violence to Children".[6]

3.6 We recommend, therefore, that the various agencies concerned should take all possible steps to identify the needs of the child. Where the family situation warrants it they should provide appropriate support to help it through periods of temporary strain and crisis. The aim should be to try to improve the quality of care provided for children and, where necessary, to supplement care and education for those considered to be "vulnerable" or "at risk". In the majority of cases it will be in the child's best interests to attempt to prevent the disintegration of the family unit.

3.7 If we accept the primacy of the family in this way and consider how statutory agencies might help, the role of the health visitor in promoting the care and development of very young children is very important. Initially the health visitor is in a position to assess the circumstances prevailing in a family and to determine whether these are likely to be prejudicial to the future well-being not only of the newborn infant but also of any other children in the home. Although the appropriate response to any problem may require collaboration with, or the help of, other professionals, it is often through health visitors that the need for support in a family becomes apparent. Health visitors must continue to be aware of their wider responsibility towards the whole family and their expertise and potential contribution to the early identification of need must be recognised and responded to by those charged with the delivery of services to children and their parents.

HELP THROUGH THE SCHOOL

3.8 The school has continuous contact with the child and his family over many years. It is a controlled environment concerned not just with the transmission of knowledge, ideas, values and specific skills which a child will require in later life, but with the development of the whole child. It is in the school that previously undetected social or emotional problems, as well as educational deficiencies, can appear. Apart from its primary role in education the school is a base for a number of existing services such as the education welfare service, the school psychological service and the school medical service: in recent years the pastoral role of the school has been developed and there has been an increased recognition of the need for a supportive atmosphere and for curricula which are relevant to children's needs.

---

6. Cmnd 7123, 1978 Paragraphs 11–18.

3.9 There are few schools in Northern Ireland which do not provide pastoral care and significantly large numbers of teachers are obtaining extra qualifications in counselling. The school counsellor's role now extends to the provision of help for children and adolescents who have developmental problems or who are undergoing a temporary crisis; to the early identification of educational, emotional or behavioural abnormality; to the referral of cases for specialist treatment; to the provision of support to teachers dealing with difficult children; and to the fostering of links between parents and the school. We consider that the formal recognition of the pastoral role of the school through school counsellors was a significant and timely development in the education and care of children. It is essential that arrangements should exist which not only provide an early warning system for children with educational, emotional or social problems, but which also ensure a pattern of vigilant and continuous care and we are convinced that the education service, by virtue of its involvement with children up to and beyond the school leaving age, is in a unique position to provide the focus for such arrangements.

HELP THROUGH THE COMMUNITY

3.10 Although the school and the family are the main bases for child development and will be the focus for formal intervention by the various agencies in providing support for children and their parents, the community in which they live can also make an important contribution towards lessening the pressures on children and in providing support for the more vulnerable members of society. It is important, therefore, to attempt to harness the resources of the community to assist families in coming together to care for their children in need. The provision of community support in this way should strengthen the family and enable it to make a more useful contribution to the community of which it is a part.

3.11 This might be achieved by the local community supplementing the provision of after-school activities or in the development of area projects. Local community groups would have an important role to play. The involvement of parents and local residents in such schemes might serve to reduce the necessity for formal intervention by the statutory services and would increase the sense of community identity. The Youth Service in Northern Ireland has increasingly brought together statutory and voluntary agencies including the churches in a concerted attempt to provide for the needs of young people. The various youth organisations in Northern Ireland now involve some 10,000 adult volunteers and have about 120,000 young persons between the ages of 10 and 20 in membership. This represents about one-third of the age group. Complementary to the valuable work of the Youth Service are the excellent recreational and sporting facilities being provided by district councils throughout Northern Ireland.

3.12 The community has some responsibility for the environment in which children are required to live and the importance of the environment to the development of children should be clearly recognised. Not only could the environment be enhanced but opportunities for crime and vandalism could be reduced by judicious design, planning and organisation: for example, by making public facilities more open to surveillance and more resistant to vandalism, reducing the temptation and opportunity for theft in shops geared to the impulse buyer, making cars harder to steal, and so on.

3.13 It is the responsibility of the community to create a sympathetic climate within which professional help may be offered to children who are in need or who have particular problems. There must be a willingness on the part of the community to accept that children hitherto perceived as disruptive, deviant or difficult, can very often be helped cope with their problems without recourse to exceptional measures. There is much to be gained from neighbourhood support for families in need and from community-based schemes to interest and support young people.

HELP THROUGH STATUTORY ACTION— A CO-ORDINATED APPROACH

3.14 In seeking a comprehensive and integrated approach to providing help for children, we have emphasised the important roles of the family, the school and the community. We recognise, however, that many children will still require help which can only be provided by the statutory agencies. These agencies necessarily focus on specific aspects of child development and our strategy depends largely on a more co-ordinated approach to children's needs. There must be some formal framework through which the various agencies can come together to review and co-ordinate their activities.

3.15 We propose a dual system of co-ordinating teams, in schools and at district level. We refer to them as School-based Care Teams and District Child Care Teams.

School-based Care Teams

3.16 The school is central to the identification of problems facing many children. The teacher is often the first person to become aware that a child is in need of help, although the child's needs may extend beyond those which can be met from within the educational sector. This is particularly so when the difficulties experienced by a child lie primarily within the family, and social work support for the whole family is required. Clearly it is unrealistic to expect teachers to act as social workers, nor would we wish them to. The welfare of the individual child will be served best by a co-operative approach involving not just the education services but the social services and any other agency or service such as the Youth Service which might contribute to the resolution of the problem at hand. We recommend, therefore, the creation of a school-based forum in which the appropriate counsellor, the education welfare officer, the educational psychologist and the social worker familiar with the catchment area of the school might combine to consider the problems of children within their charge. The School-based Care Team should be able to draw upon the expertise and advice of the police and Probation Service and preferably should include a representative from those agencies as occasion demands.

3.17 There should be a free exchange of information among the agencies involved in the multi-disciplinary team. Problems manifesting themselves in the school, in the home or in the community, whether they first come to the attention of the education authorities, the social services or the police should be referred to the School-based Care Team for discussion and consideration of what help, if any, each of the agencies might provide for the child and his family to help solve the problem. Parents should be kept informed at all stages and involved where possible in any action taken.

3.18 The School-based Care Teams should not have executive functions; each agency should be responsible for the action required of it in an individual case. The team should provide the focus for assessing the response of the child and his family to the help or treatment offered. The acceptance of help or support should be voluntary on the part of the child and his parents, though compulsory intervention on the basis of a court order would be possible if the circumstances warranted such a step. Suitable arrangements for reporting back on progress should be devised.

3.19 The specific aim of our proposals is the early identification and resolution of the problems facing children and young people and the construction of an integrated programme of help for children in need from the pre-school stage. The multi-disciplinary teams should be based initially in those secondary schools where the need is most apparent and should provide a service to those schools and, most importantly, to such satellite primary schools as demonstrate a need for such services. The primary school is the key to the identification of many problems among children and young people which, if left to the secondary school stage, may become intractable. The task of alerting social services, or any other appropriate agency, should lie with the school principal who may delegate this function to the home school liaison, or other, teacher.

3.20 We hope that our proposals will go some way towards resolving many of the problems which come to notice in the school including the problem of persistent absenteeism.

District Child Care Teams

3.21 Representatives of statutory agencies concerned with the interests of children, and operating in the same area, should meet together in a recognised forum to consider the best course of action in dealing with identified problems. We consider that this could best be achieved by teams operating at district level, based on the social services districts.

3.22 These teams should be under the chairmanship of the District Social Services Officer because of his statutory responsibilities for children in need. They should include representation from the education services, the Youth Service and, as occasion demands, the Probation Service. As required, contact should be maintained with community service officers in the district councils and with the voluntary sector.

3.23 The teams, which we regard as of key importance, should be responsible for the co-ordination and oversight of the preventive and supportive services within each district. They should combine the supervision of the school-based teams with a strategic role in reviewing resources, easing inter-agency co-operation and monitoring the success of programmes of intervention. They would review particularly difficult cases, especially those involving removal from home or loss of parental rights, and co-ordinate the provision of information to the courts as required.

3.24 The multi-disciplinary approach to children's problems which we envisage can only work where the professions concerned are prepared to work together in an atmosphere of trust and understanding and to exchange information and ideas for the benefit of the individual child. Co-operation will not be achieved through legislation or by administrative dictate but by sensitivity to the problems of young people and the development of complementary, rather than competing, responses. These aims might be furthered through the introduction of joint in-service courses for teachers, social workers and education welfare officers and by greater recognition in initial training of the inter-disciplinary element in the work of the respective agencies.

3.25 With the creation of these teams and the deliberate pursuit of a policy of early identification of needs, care must be taken to avoid labelling children as deviant, abnormal, troublesome or delinquent. So far as possible children should be dealt with by the services normally available to all children and the child should not be segregated from his family, school, community or peer group.

HELP THROUGH STATUTORY ACTION—PREVENTIVE WORK

3.26 Apart from coming together at school and district level, the agencies already have certain powers and responsibilities which, if effectively employed, could contribute significantly to preventing problems before they arise or in dealing with problems once they have arisen. We round off this chapter by looking briefly at three areas where statutory agencies can help to protect and enhance a child's interests.

Provision for the Under Fives

3.27 There is little doubt that the early, formative years have an immense bearing on a child's future development. We were therefore pleased to note the publication last year of the policy paper on day care and education for the under fives[7]. We are convinced that a significant improvement in the level of provision for the under fives in Northern Ireland is essential as part of our strategy for help.

3.28 The policy paper referred to pre-school care for children in the following terms: ". . . one advantage of pre-school care is that it can often provide vital relief for parents who face the cumulative pressures of poverty, sub-standard housing, family problems and general social and economic insecurity." The relief for parents in these circumstances is perhaps only matched by the corresponding benefit to the child to be derived from a changed and more stimulating environment. Day care provision is particularly important for the children of single parents and working mothers.

3.29 Without the provision of adequate day care arrangements for the under fives there is a grave danger that a number of children will continue to suffer neglect, however inadvertent this might be, and to experience some form of social, emotional or intellectual impairment. Compensatory care and education for these children should be a priority.

Legislative Powers

3.30 In preparing a strategy of help, we have been aware that the Health and Social Services Boards have statutory obligations to safeguard the interests of children and are able to take steps to assist families and children in certain

7. See paragraph 2.8.

circumstances. The Boards have a duty ". . . to make available such advice, guidance and assistance as may promote the welfare of children by diminishing the need to receive children into or keep them in care . . . or to bring children before a court; . . .".[8] We have gained the impression, however, that these preventive powers have been narrowly interpreted, few resources being allocated to preventive work and attention being concentrated on families or children "at risk" or "in need".

3.31 While it would be wrong to advocate a general widening of these preventive powers at a time when financial resources are limited, and thereby to impose on Boards an unrealistic requirement, we would see merit in some re-drafting of the statutory provisions so as to encourage preventive work on a wider basis than at present. We acknowledge, however, that a balance must be struck between creating a demand-responsive, universalist service for all families and children, and a restrictive legislative provision which might continue to stultify preventive work.

Intermediate Treatment

3.32 In the context of community involvement with young people, we have studied with interest the development of "intermediate treatment" schemes in Great Britain. "Intermediate treatment" is a term which covers social work with children and young people, seeking to improve their quality of life through providing community–based opportunities. It involves a range of activities, recreational or otherwise, at present largely directed towards the child who may have appeared before the courts or who may be at risk of doing so. In England and Wales participation in such schemes can be one of the conditions attached to a supervision order[9].

3.33 We feel strongly, however, that participation in such schemes should be achieved on a voluntary basis, with the agreement of the individual and his family. It seems inappropriate, given the nature and objectives of such schemes, to use them as a sanction. While supporting the concept of what has come to be known as intermediate treatment we do not recommend that it should be made compulsory.

3.34 The objectives of intermediate treatment schemes must be clearly defined and careful thought must be given to the selection of appropriate children. The programmes are essentially locally–based and their flexible nature has been well illustrated in a recent publication entitled "Intermediate Treatment: 28 Choices"[10]. In Northern Ireland, the Health and Social Services Boards, the Probation Service, training schools and the Youth Service in conjunction with the Education and Library Boards, are developing a wide range of activities incorporated in intermediate treatment programmes. We would encourage these initiatives and recommend that additional resources should be allocated for their expansion. We do not consider that such programmes can be regarded as a panacea for delinquent or anti-social behaviour; indeed any effective evaluation of their "success" seems unrealistic. We accept, however, that such an approach can meet the needs of many children who, left to their own devices, might otherwise require much more intensive support at a later stage.

8. Section 164 of the 1968 Act.
9. Section 12 Children and Young Persons Act 1969.
10. Department of Health and Social Security 1977.

3.35 We are recommending a strategy of help for all children and their families. The emphasis should be on early identification of problems. Attempts should be made to meet these by reinforcing the key role of the family and by a co-ordinated response from all of the statutory and voluntary agencies concerned with the interests and welfare of children, complemented by support from the wider community.

3.36 So far we have tried to set the problems in perspective and have proposed a broad framework for future policy. Next we consider those cases where, for one reason or another, the family fails to provide children with adequate care and protection.

4—Care and Protection

4.1 Most families will succeed in coping with the problems of their growing children and the aim of any system must be to enable more to do so, and lessen the possibility of compulsory intervention. We regard the removal of a child from his family and the loss of parental rights as a significant incursion into the affairs of the family, to be tolerated only when the welfare of the child itself is at grave risk and can reasonably be safeguarded in no other way. The emphasis, therefore, should be on keeping children with their families wherever possible and every effort should be made to avoid taking them into care. The need for the State to intervene, however, in order to protect children has unfortunately been apparent all too often, and through no fault of their own many children have to be taken away from their families and cared for by statutory or voluntary agencies. In this chapter, we propose modified procedures for dealing with children in need of care, protection or control, and we go on to discuss briefly some of the forms of care available to them, and to consider the adequacy of the existing legislation to protect children.

4.2 A child in need of care can be received voluntarily into care or can be committed compulsorily to care. In Northern Ireland a child can be received voluntarily into the care of a Health and Social Services Board where it appears that the child has neither parent nor guardian, has been and remains abandoned by his parents or guardian, is lost, or his parents or guardian are either temporarily (perhaps through illness), or permanently, prevented from providing for his proper accommodation, maintenance and upbringing. In these circumstances it is the duty of the Board to receive the child into care.[11] Many children, however, who are found by a court to be in need of care, protection or control have to be committed to care and the circumstances[12] cover a range of situations—for example the child may be exposed to moral danger or may face unnecessary suffering. Broadly speaking, a child or young person is deemed to be in need of care, protection or control if ". . . he is not receiving such care, protection or control as a good parent may reasonably be expected to give; or if he is beyond the control of his parent or guardian."[13] The distinction between being voluntarily received into care and compulsory committal to care is important and will arise again when the question of parental rights is being discussed.[14] We turn first, however, to considering the procedures through which children can be committed to care.

THE JUDICIAL PROCESS

4.3 The juvenile court in Northern Ireland currently deals both with cases requiring care, protection or control and cases involving the alleged commission of an offence; often both types of case are dealt with on the same day and by the same magistrate. In this way children requiring protection are dealt with in the same forum as young people who may have committed offences and the court is conducted in the same adversarial manner for both types of case.

---

11. Section 103 of 1968 Act.
12. Sections 93–95 of 1968 Act.
13. Section 93.
14. See paragraphs 4.26–4.28.

4.4   Bearing in mind the need to safeguard the interests of children, we have considered the arguments for and against retaining the existing system. There was support for a family court which would deal with various matters relating to the family and to children including the transfer of parental rights, the committal of children to care and adoption orders, as well as wider "family" issues such as matrimonial proceedings. We examined the use of family courts in other countries and considered the arguments advanced by the Finer Committee[15]. Although in the long run a family court may provide the best forum for dealing with these cases, the issues involved in the establishment of a family court are beyond our remit. While sympathising with the school of thought that a single court should deal with all family matters, we recognise that a family court could be heavily occupied with adult business. It is arguable that a separate forum for juveniles, appropriately operated, would be in the best interests of a child. We do not see a need to suggest radical change in the courts system in Northern Ireland at this stage. We see merit in retaining a judicial setting to safeguard fully the rights of children, and our recommendations are aimed at improving existing procedures.

4.5   While advocating the retention of the juvenile court, we wish to ensure that care proceedings will be divorced from offence proceedings and that the general atmosphere in which the problems facing children in need of care, protection or control are considered will be improved and made more easily understood[16]. Every effort should be made to ensure that the child and his parents understand what is happening and why it is happening. The lay panel should be retained but, in care proceedings, the lay members would be carefully chosen for their expertise or interest in such cases. We recommend in addition that appropriate training should be given to the lay members.

4.6   We consider it essential that a child should be adequately represented in legal proceedings. In any case where there could be a conflict between the interest of a child and that of his parent or guardian, we recommend that a guardian ad litem, drawn from a panel of suitably-qualified people, should be appointed to safeguard the child's interest. This would bring the law in Northern Ireland into line with that in England and Wales[17].

4.7   We examined closely the arguments for the appointment of child advocates, in addition to, or instead of, guardians ad litem. Some respondents to the Consultative Document thought that the child should be represented in legal proceedings by either a lawyer or a social worker, or by a new type of professional who might ideally combine the attributes of both the lawyer and the social worker. We considered too the merits of setting up a separate Office of the Child Advocate, or an extension of the duties of the Official Solicitor in juvenile proceedings. On balance, however, we would recommend that a guardian ad litem should be appointed by the court in every case where there is any doubt as to whether the interests of the child are being adequately protected, and a child should have the right to separate legal representation. As legal aid is available to both the parents and the child in care proceedings[18]

---

15. Report of the Committee on One Parent Families. 1974. Cmnd 5629.
16. The juvenile court in offence proceedings is discussed more fully in Chapter 6 (paragraphs 6.12 et seq).
17. cf. section 64 of the Children Act 1975.
18. For the position in criminal proceedings see paragraph 6.43.

in Northern Ireland we do not feel it necessary to make specific recommendations in this context.

4.8 In order to ensure adequate consideration of each case, we recommend that the care authority responsible for bringing the proceedings should be required to present a report to the court setting out the grounds for committal to care and indicating the likely form of care proposed for the child. Such reports should normally be made available to the various parties to the proceedings and to their legal representatives.

4.9 Having recommended the establishment of a separate juvenile court in care proceedings, with adequate and readily available representation for the child, we need now to consider the powers of that court and the methods of disposal available to it. Our proposals do not coincide with the systems currently operating in England and Wales or in Scotland, but it is worth examining those systems in order to place our own recommendations in a wider context.

4.10 In England and Wales provision is made for two types of court order, the care order and the supervision order[19]. The care order has the effect of committing a child to the care of a local authority, and that authority, not the juvenile court, is responsible for deciding how the child should be cared for: for example, boarded out with foster parents, maintained in a community home or in a home run by a voluntary organisation, or returned to his own home. The care order can be made in respect of offenders or non-offenders. Under a supervision order the child remains at home, subject to the supervision of the relevant local authority or a probation officer.

4.11 In Scotland the position is different.[20] The Scottish courts deal only with the most serious criminal cases; the children's hearings being responsible for all care proceedings, and the disposal of a case being a matter for the children's panel system. Certain powers of disposal reside in the reporter but, where compulsory measures of care are required, he refers the case to the panel to determine the most appropriate course of action so as to further the best interests of the child. The panel can order supervision in the community by the local authority social services department, or supervision with a residential requirement, or any other condition considered appropriate.

4.12 The existing position in Northern Ireland is that, in committing children to care[21], the juvenile court can either make a fit person order, a supervision order, or a training school order[22] or require the parents or guardian to enter into a recognisance to exercise proper care and guardianship. Where a child is voluntarily in care, rights over the child can be obtained by a parental rights order[23]. As in the rest of the United Kingdom, there is provision under which, in emergency situations, children can be taken to a place of safety.[24]

---

19. Section 1(3) of the 1969 Act.
20. Part III of the Social Work (Scotland) Act 1968: see also our discussion of the Scottish system in Chapter II and Appendix III of the Consultative Document.
21. Section 95 of the 1968 Act.
22. The use of training school orders now and in the future is discussed in Chapter 6.
23. Section 104 of the 1968 Act.
24. Sections 99 and 100 of the 1968 Act.

4.13 Following the principle that there should be minimal interference in family matters consistent with safeguarding the welfare of the child we propose three main types of order. These are a place of safety order, to provide for the removal of a child in an emergency from an environment of physical, mental or moral danger; a supervision order, where a child may be supervised in the home setting; and a care order, which would include most of the characteristics of the fit person order and which would carry with it the loss of parental rights. There may be a need for a separate parental rights order in some cases. There would no longer be a training school order since any children convicted of a criminal offence would be accommodated in the single custodial unit we propose.[25]

Place of Safety Orders

4.14 The 1968 Act[26] provides for a constable, or any person authorised by a court or by a justice of the peace, to take to a place of safety ". . . any child or young person in respect of whom any of the offences mentioned in Schedule 1 has been or is believed to have been committed, . . .": traditionally places of safety have included remand homes, police stations and hospitals. A child admitted to a hospital, perhaps for routine examination before any suspicions arise regarding possible abuse, is already in a place of safety and cannot, therefore, be taken. We recommend that this apparent defect in the legislation should be remedied.

4.15 A child can be taken to a place of safety under the 1968 Act either by authorised persons acting under warrant or by a constable acting without warrant: a child can also take refuge in a place of safety. In all cases the child must be brought before the juvenile court. The existing time limits for bringing such proceedings vary according to the method whereby the child came to be in the place of safety. Where he has been brought there without warrant, or has taken refuge there, he must be brought before a juvenile court or a justice of the peace within eight days. We consider that the detention or retention of a child apart from his family is a very serious matter and we recommend that the legislation should provide for more urgent judicial action where no warrant has been issued.

4.16 We looked also at the legal requirements in Northern Ireland to notify a parent or guardian that his child has been taken to a place of safety. Under the 1968 Act[27], a parent or guardian may be required to attend the court before which the child is brought. It is theoretically possible for a child removed to a place of safety to be released within the time limit set in the Act[28] without being brought before a court and, therefore, the parent or guardian need never be notified of the position. This is different from the situation in England and Wales as the 1969 Act[29] requires "such steps as are practicable" to be taken for notifying the parent or guardian of the child's detention and of the reason for it. In Scotland a constable removing a child to a place of safety without a warrant is required to notify the reporter forthwith[30]. We recommend, therefore, that a specific requirement to notify parents as quickly as possible be included in any future legislation relating to places of safety.

---

25. Paragraph 6.30.
26. Section 99.
27. Section 52(2).
28. Section 100(3).
29. Section 28 of the 1969 Act.
30. Under section 37(2) of the Social Work (Scotland) Act 1968.

Supervision Orders

4.17 Taking a child into care is a serious step which should not be undertaken lightly. In many cases an alternative should be tried, especially where a child is difficult to control but where the home conditions are not so bad as to justify committal to care. In such circumstances, supervision by a social worker, or, in cases of persistent school absenteeism, an education welfare officer, may meet the situation. Wherever possible, such supervision should be agreed with the parents. If voluntary agreement, given perhaps when a family is under stress, is not sufficient to ensure effective supervision then we consider that it should be possible for a Health and Social Services Board, or an Education and Library Board, to seek a supervision order from the juvenile court responsible for care proceedings. Similarly, the court would be asked to adjudicate on cases where parental agreement was not forthcoming.

4.18 A supervision order would be made by the court in care proceedings for a determinate period, but not for more than three years, subject to the qualification that it would not have effect after attainment of age 18, nor beyond the upper limit of compulsory school age in truancy cases. The duty of the supervisor would be to befriend and advise the child.

4.19 Before a supervision order is sought, the case would have been discussed fully within the District Child Care Team. Either a Health and Social Services Board or an Education and Library Board could seek the order; the Education and Library Board would do so in the case of persistent absenteeism from school, and the nominated supervisor in these cases would normally be an education welfare officer. If supervision proved ineffective, the child would have to be brought back to the court. We propose that in doing so in truancy cases the Education and Library Board should give notice of its intention to the Health and Social Services Board and that Board should give a report in writing, or appear before the court, in order to assist the court in its consideration of whether or not it would be appropriate to make a care order.

Care Orders

4.20 The care order would give the Health and Social Services Board parental rights over a child, including the right to decide how best to care for him. Such an order would be the ultimate option available to a court in care proceedings. The grounds on which a care order would be sought would, subject to our recommendations below[31], be those under which court proceedings can currently be taken in Northern Ireland under section 93 (fit person orders) of the 1968 Act, viz:—

he is falling into bad associations or is exposed to moral danger; or

the lack of care, protection or guidance is likely to cause him unnecessary suffering or seriously to affect his health or proper development; or

any of the offences mentioned in Schedule 1 (to the Act) has been committed in respect of him or in respect of a child or young person who is a member of the same household; or

he is a member of the same household as a person who has been convicted of such an offence in respect of a child or young person; or

---

31. Paragraphs 4.46 and 4.48.

the child or young person is a female member of a household a member of which has committed or attempted to commit an offence under section 1 of the Punishment of Incest Act 1908; and

in any of these circumstances he is not receiving such care, protection and guidance as a good parent may reasonably be expected to give; or

he is beyond the control of his parent or guardian.

We recommend the retention of these grounds for the making of a care order, together with the following additional grounds:—

the breakdown of a supervision order; and

the provisions set out in section 1 of the 1969 Act in England and Wales relating to neglect and ill-treatment.

4.21 One of the main differences between the Northern Ireland care order and that currently available in England and Wales would be the fact that the Northern Ireland order could only be made in care proceedings. It would not be possible for the juvenile court dealing with criminal cases to make a care order.

4.22 Before a Health and Social Services Board would seek a care order every effort should have been made to keep the child or young person out of care. In doing so the District Child Care Team would have an important role to play. It is in this forum that the Board will be able to consider with the other agencies involved the best course of action in each case. A care order would not be sought lightly but only after voluntary arrangements, or perhaps the use of a supervision order, had been considered.

4.23 In our proposed system, a care order could be applied for by a Health and Social Services Board or an authorised person. At present the only persons authorised in Northern Ireland are officers of the National Society for the Prevention of Cruelty to Children.

4.24 If the court decides to make an order, the child would be given into the care of a Health and Social Services Board. Once committed it would be a matter for the Board to decide the most appropriate form of care, whether residential care, boarding out or allowing him home under supervision. In granting or refusing an order, the court would apply the usual standards of proof which obtain in civil proceedings and every case would accordingly be treated with due legal process. A care order would continue in force until the young person attained the age of 18 and we recommend that provision should be made for a court review of a care order at least every three years.

4.25 In addition to this judicial review, regulations should provide for a working review every six months of all children in care, including consideration of the need to continue the order. This review would be carried out by the Health and Social Services Board in conjunction, as appropriate, with the other members of the District Child Care Team. As at present, revocation of the order could be sought at any time.

Parental Rights Orders

4.26 When parents are unable, either temporarily or permanently, to look after their children, they may make voluntary arrangements for a Health and Social Services Board to receive them into care; where the parents or guardians are absent, the Board is under a duty to receive them into care. Circumstances may arise when, having been received into care, it may become necessary for a Board to seek fuller powers of control over the child and this is done by applying for a parental rights order.

4.27 We recommend that this type of order be retained in Northern Ireland. We considered the merits of merging the parental rights order with the care order but the grounds for seeking these two types of order differ and there are certain practical problems, including the possibility that rights may need to be taken from only one parent rather than both, which would arise from such a merger. On balance, therefore, we decided that two separate methods for obtaining parental rights should be retained. This will mean that the position in Northern Ireland will continue to differ from that in England and Wales. Whereas parental rights can be assumed in England and Wales by means of a resolution made by a local authority[32] (unless the parent formally objects, in which case the resolution lapses unless the matter is brought to the court for decision), in Northern Ireland it will still be necessary to seek an order of the court in all cases. We consider the assumption of parental rights such a significant incursion into the affairs of a family that it demands full consideration by a court in every case.

4.28 We considered the new provisions governing the assumption of parental rights introduced in England and Wales by the Children Act 1975. Under that Act, a local authority may assume parental rights if a child has been voluntarily in care for at least three years[33], and a voluntary organisation will be able to apply to a local authority for parental rights in respect of a child voluntarily in their care[34]. As no evidence was adduced to us we decided against recommending the introduction of similar provisions in Northern Ireland.

4.29 Where a child is taken into the care of a Health and Social Services Board, the Board has a duty to exercise its powers with respect to him ". . . so as to further his best interests, and to afford him opportunity for the proper development of his character and abilities."[35] This is a different requirement from that contained in the 1975 Children Act[36] which provides, inter alia:—

> "In reaching any decision relating to a child in their care, a local authority shall give first consideration to the need to safeguard and promote the welfare of the child throughout his childhood; and shall so far as practicable ascertain the wishes and feelings of the child regarding the decision and give due consideration to them, having regard to his age and understanding."

In Great Britain, however, difficulties have arisen over the interpretation of the term "first consideration", in some instances the expression having been regarded as a weighting factor, that is, more weight should be given to the child's welfare than to anything else. The difficulty is that there is no guidance as to just what weight should be given. It is generally agreed that, if the child's welfare were intended to outweigh all other considerations, then the word "paramount" might have been used in the legislation, but we understand that this was deliberately avoided. We believe, therefore, that a more relevant

---

32. Section 2 Children Act 1948.
33. Section 57 Children Act 1975.
34. Section 60 Children Act 1975 (not yet in force).
35. Section 113 of the 1968 Act.
36. Section 59 of the 1975 Act.

expression to use in this connection is "full consideration", this term indicating that the child's welfare will be given all the weight it is capable of having in the eyes of a reasonable person, given the circumstances of the particular case. We would also support the need to ascertain the wishes and feelings of the child regarding any decision and would recommend that the relevant provision be re-drafted along these lines.

PROVISION OF CARE

4.30 In deciding how best to meet the needs of children in their care, the Health and Social Services Boards will need to have available a range of services and facilities. Each case must be considered on its merits and the form of care matched to the needs of the individual child. This will require adequate assessment procedures and the availability of a range of caring options. While every effort should be made to keep children where possible with their families, a large number of children in care will still require substitute parenting through fostering or residential care. Since reorganisation of the personal social services in 1973, on average each year 44% of children in care have been boarded out and 44% placed in residential care. We now look briefly at these two methods of caring for children.

Fostering

4.31 Fostering offers an alternative to residential care which is more closely related to normal family life and offers greater flexibility in approach. It can be used, for example, to cater for children who are difficult to place, and we have noted a pilot project on the use of professional foster parents being developed by Dr. Barnardo's. We understand that the Health and Social Services Boards intend to draw up schemes to encourage specifically the fostering of older children. Foster care, however, is demanding and we consider that greater emphasis needs to be placed on the training and selection of foster parents.

4.32 Under the 1968 Act[37], boarding out with foster parents is the preferred method of placement for children in care. While we would encourage the development of fostering services, we do not think that the legislation should continue to favour boarding-out in preference to other forms of care. Boarding-out is a form of care which may be suitable for some, but not for others. We recommend, therefore, that the statutory bias in favour of boarding-out should be removed.

4.33 A sub-committee of the Central Personal Social Services Advisory Committee set up in 1978 has been examining the current arrangements for the boarding-out of children and will be making detailed recommendations for the improvement of foster care in Northern Ireland.

4.34 Our Consultative Document drew attention to the particular concern aroused where natural parents reclaim a foster child, perhaps after a lengthy period in foster care. We would support the introduction of a statutory delay in the removal of children from care, or from a foster family, as provided for in section 56 of the Children Act 1975. This provision makes it an offence for any person, including the parents of the child, to remove any child who has been in the care of a local authority throughout the preceding six months, unless he has the consent of the local authority or has given at least 28 days' notice of his intention to do so.

---

37. Section 114.

4.35 Custodianship orders[38], introduced in Part II of the 1975 Act, would give foster parents greater rights to the child in their care, but the provisions are as yet untried and no strong case has been made for their use in Northern Ireland. Accordingly we would not advocate the introduction of custodianship orders in relation to fostering at present but recommend further consideration when there has been sufficient time to monitor their effectiveness in Great Britain. Consideration of custodianship as an alternative to adoption is a separate question and has been raised in the Review Group's consultative paper "Adoption of Children in Northern Ireland".

Residential Care

4.36 Much has been written about residential care and we cannot hope to cover all the ground in this Report. We will focus, therefore, on certain aspects of residential care which seem important or which have been brought to our attention. The main areas of concern are the need for adequate assessment procedures, the need for a greater range of residential provision, the provision of education for children in residential care, the need to take full cognisance of the role of the voluntary sector in providing residential accommodation, and the means of recruiting and retaining trained residential care staff. The implications of our recommendations for the future of the existing residential facilities for young offenders are discussed more fully in Chapter 6[39].

4.37 Greater emphasis needs to be placed on ensuring that the needs of a child are accurately identified by some form of professional assessment before selecting the form of care which appears to be the most appropriate. Although assessment has traditionally been carried out in a residential setting, assessment at home, or by attendance at a special unit, should be further explored. It has been argued that residential assessment does not provide a valid picture since the removal of the child from his natural environment creates an artificial situation in which he is unlikely to behave normally. While there is a need for more assessment centres, therefore, there is also a strong case for the use of day centres and peripatetic assessment teams.

4.38 The lack of variety in residential provision has been highlighted in recent years by changes in the concept of residential care and a greater awareness of the needs of particular groups of children. Historically the planning of facilities in Northern Ireland by eight separate welfare authorities was not conducive to a comprehensive strategy, and the Health and Social Services Boards are still in the process of identifying areas of need and planning facilities accordingly. Many of the respondents to the Consultative Document mentioned the grave shortage of places in residential hostels for adolescents. Hostels provide an intermediate form of care between the children's home or training school and the independence of living in the community, where a young person, because of an unsatisfactory home, is unable to return to live with parents. We think there should be more hostel places. We also see a need for a residential unit for young people who present behavioural problems which cannot be catered for adequately in the normal children's home, for example, disruptive young

---

38. Custodianship is an extension of guardianship law, based on Recommendation 21 of the Report of the Departmental Committee on the Adoption of Children (Houghton Report. Cmnd 5107. 1972), which provides for the granting of legal custody of a child to relatives already caring for him, and to foster parents.
39. Paragraph 6.33 et seq.

people. It is uncertain how great a demand there would be for this facility but the evidence available indicates that, without such provision, some disturbed adolescents are being accommodated quite inappropriately in other forms of residential care. It may be feasible to provide this type of accommodation on a regional basis.

4.39 We would stress the need to make adequate and appropriate provision for the education of children while in residential care. For those who reside in children's homes and hostels, educational facilities should be available within the community in local schools, where the facilities for remedial classes and teachers will also be available if required. For those few young people who, for their own safety or the protection of the community, have to be retained in secure accommodation there should be education provided on the premises. In general, such education should be provided by teachers from the community coming into the unit each day.

4.40 We wish to acknowledge the unique and vital role played by voluntary organisations in the provision of residential child care facilities in Northern Ireland. Later in the Report[40] we recommend that any administrative arrangements designed to improve co-ordination should fully recognise and accommodate the views of these bodies with a view to cementing a more effective partnership with statutory interests. Efforts should be made to avoid unnecessary duplication in the provision of residential facilities and the contribution which can be made by the voluntary sector should be recognised.

4.41 In the Consultative Document we noted that many of the existing voluntary bodies are closely linked to a particular religious denomination. In our opinion future provision should follow ways which preserve the principle of voluntary involvement, particularly by church-based bodies, whilst avoiding the rigidities inherent in strict denominational segregation, especially for specialist units. This is already the practice in statutory, and in some voluntary, homes and in Lisnevin School, where experience has demonstrated that the approach can work satisfactorily. While conscious of the merits in bringing children of different backgrounds together, and favouring an integrated approach, we recognise that progress in this respect can only realistically be made when the climate is favourable. Nevertheless we regard this as a desirable long-term objective.

4.42 It is important to ensure that the quality of the staff involved in residential care is high. We are aware that there is an unacceptable level of untrained staff in residential homes and we recommend that residential care staff should be encouraged to undertake appropriate training.

4.43 The appointment of independent persons, known as visitors, to advise and befriend children in care over five years of age was introduced in England and Wales by the 1969 Act[41]. If a child has not been allowed to leave residential care for three months to attend an educational institution or go to work, the social services department, concerned that communication between him and his parent or guardian is too infrequent, can appoint a visitor; or if a child has not lived with or visited, or been visited by, either of his parents or his guardian during the preceding twelve months, an independent visitor has to be

---

40. Paragraph 8.4.
41. Section 24.

appointed. A visitor is independent of the caring authority and must satisfy conditions prescribed by regulations. Duties include visiting, advising and befriending and the visitor has the right to apply on the child's behalf for variation or discharge of a care order. The need for such appointments in Northern Ireland has been mentioned in the written evidence received and we would support the proposals as an additional safeguard for a small number of children in care whose parents or guardians are taking little or no interest in them. Accordingly, we recommend the introduction of a similar provision in Northern Ireland designed to cover all children in care irrespective of their age.

PROTECTIVE PROVISIONS

4.44 In the remainder of this chapter we look at the legislation which affords protection to children. We make some proposals with a view to averting child abuse and we seek some changes in the law relating to the registration of child-minding premises and to the employment of children.

Child Abuse

4.45 In recent years a great deal of publicity has been given to non-accidental injury to children and from time to time individual cases have made headline news. The Department of Health and Social Services has issued a number of circulars[42] offering guidance on the identification and management of cases. In 1977 the Select Committee on Violence in the Family published a report[43] on violence to children which, although it did not extend specifically to Northern Ireland, provided a useful conspectus of current thinking in Great Britain on this topic. Copies of the recommendations of the Select Committee were widely circulated to interested agencies in Northern Ireland and their responses to this consultative exercise were incorporated in a further circular[44] from the Department of Health and Social Services which was issued in August 1978 following publication of the White Paper "Violence to Children"[45]. Health and Social Services Boards and other agencies were encouraged to take the recommendations of the Select Committee, and the Government's response, into account in the planning of their services relating to children. We welcome the attention which has been given to these problems.

4.46 A number of legislative issues, however, arise in connection with child abuse and we propose certain amendments to the existing law. Section 20 of the 1968 Act, for example, deals with neglect and ill-treatment but, while referring to mental derangement, does not refer specifically to verbal and psychological abuse. In view of the need to protect children against emotional abuse as well as physical injury some restatement of the law in this area is recommended.

4.47 Legislation in the past has tended to operate on the basis of protecting the child once he has been abused or neglected. We consider that it will have to move towards authorising action to prevent abuse or neglect. In doing so, it may be necessary to lay more emphasis on the needs of the child and less on the rights and expectations of parents. We consider that in cases of doubt the balance should always be in favour of the child. With this in mind, some

42. Circular HSS (Gen 1) 1/75: "Non-accidental Injury to Children"; Circular HSS (CCB) 1/78: "Child Abuse".
43. Session 1976–77. Report 329–i. HMSO.
44. Circular HSS (CCB) 5/78: "Violence to Children".
45. Cmnd 7123. 1978.

redefinition of the term "in need of care, protection or control" as used in section 93 of the 1968 Act is recommended. Sub-sections 2(c), (d) and (e) of this section refer to children who are members "of the same household" as another child or young person who has been the victim of certain offences, or a person who has been convicted of any such offence in respect of a child or young person.

4.48 Specific cases have come to light which cast doubt on the capacity of these provisions to protect a baby born in hospital, who technically has never been a member of the same household, but who undoubtedly would be on discharge from hospital. Accordingly, we recommend that the law be amended to take account of this situation. Similarly, the existing provision does not take account of the situation where a person who is, or would be, a member of the same household is being tried for one of the offences specified in Schedule 1 to the Act. Such a person may well be released on bail and, whereas there is a legal presumption of innocence unless and until the contrary is proved, nevertheless it is considered that any risk to the child would be unacceptable in these circumstances. Again, we recommend the existing law be amended to include in the definition of "in need of care, protection or control" any child whose household includes, or would include, a person who has been convicted of, or is presently on remand in respect of, or on trial for, any of the specified offences.

Approval of Placements and Registration of Premises

4.49 Part I of the 1968 Act regulates the circumstances in which children may be cared for in the temporary absence of their parents. It covers both situations where the parent may be physically absent for a period and seeks to make arrangements for the care and maintenance of the child during this period, and the more common childminding arrangement where the parent is regularly absent for a short period during the day. In both cases some form of statutory approval of the arrangement is required, either by way of approval of the individual placement or by registration of the appropriate premises. We do not propose that the present law be changed; indeed the register required to be kept by the Health and Social Services Boards under section 11(2) of the Act should provide a valuable reference to the available facilities in an area. We do recommend, however, that placements with a view to adoption should be governed by provisions of separate adoption law[46].

4.50 When seeking to protect the interests of children the legislators of 1968 took account of contemporary social standards and conditions. We have had to consider the legislation in the light of current norms. Attitudes towards day care for young children have changed and the variety of facilities now provided for children and young people is quite different from the situation in 1968. There is now a wide range of facilities where it could be argued that the provisions of Part I of the 1968 Act might apply but may not have been intended to apply. Examples include junior youth clubs, play-schemes and outdoor pursuit centres, whether run by statutory or voluntary bodies or by schools. Whereas schools, as defined in the Education and Libraries (Northern Ireland) Order 1972, are exempt from the registration provisions of the 1968 Act, it is not clear whether other facilities, including outdoor pursuit centres

46. See Consultative Paper on Adoption, Chapter 7.

may be similarly exempted. Where arrangements are made in leisure centres, specially for very young children and babies whilst the rest of the family takes advantage of the recreational facilities, it may be necessary to consider the standards of care offered in the context of Part I of the Act. The position of uniformed youth organisations which use premises on a regular basis might also usefully be clarified.

4.51 We appreciate the impracticability of requiring all such premises to be registered. With registration goes the right of inspection and this leads into a situation where social services personnel would be inspecting facilities unrelated to the social services. The position is complicated and it will be necessary to clarify those situations which should be exempt from control, those which should be controlled by the Department of Education or the Education and Library Boards, and those which should be controlled by the Department of Health and Social Services or the Health and Social Services Boards. We have asked the two Departments to initiate a review of the legislation in conjunction with the relevant agencies.

Employment of Children

4.52 Part III of the 1968 Act controls the employment of children and young persons. Section 37 prohibits the employment of any child:—

so long as he is under the age of 13 years; or

before the close of school hours on any day on which he is required to attend school; or

before seven o'clock in the morning or after seven o'clock in the evening on any day; or

for more than two hours on any day on which he is required to attend school; or

for more than two hours on a Sunday.

In addition, an Education and Library Board is empowered to make byelaws, subject to the approval of the Department of Health and Social Services, to place further restrictions on the employment of children.

4.53 As with the registration of premises, it is doubtful whether this legislation takes sufficiently into account changes in the pattern of life in recent years. Since the 1968 Act was passed the school-leaving age has been increased to 16 (and for some pupils this means 16 years 7 months) and so these provisions now embrace the 15–16 year-olds who may not require the same protection as younger children. There is nothing inherently wrong with children aged between 13–16 working to some extent while they are at school and to a greater extent during school holidays; legislation should not be too rigid or conflict unduly with the attidues of parents and children. It may be thought reasonable, for example, to relax the conditions of section 37 for those aged over 15, at least during school holidays. We have asked the Departments of Health and Social Services and of Education to consider whether the legislation should be amended and whether the two-tiered system of control (primary legislation resting in the Children and Young Persons Act and secondary rules being drawn up by the Education and Library Boards by way of byelaws) should remain.

26

SUMMARY

4.54 In seeking to meet the needs of children in need of care, protection and control we have recommended:—

(1) a revision of the general duty of the Health and Social Services Boards to safeguard the welfare of children;

(2) the introduction of separate sittings of the juvenile court to deal with care proceedings, requiring the careful selection and training of lay panel members;

(3) the introduction of a care order to replace the existing fit person order and training school order;

(4) the removal of the statutory bias towards fostering;

(5) some proposals to improve the quality of residential care; and

(6) some revision of the 1968 Act to counter the possibility of child abuse.

We have also asked the Departments of Health and Social Services and of Education to examine the legislation covering registration of child-minding facilities and the employment of children.

5—Welfare and Justice

5.1 In the previous chapter we discussed the need for compulsory intervention on behalf of children in need of care, protection or control. This chapter deals with one of the most fundamental questions posed in the Consultative Document[47]: should children who commit offences be dealt with as children in need of care and within a system designed to promote their welfare rather than as offenders subject to the criminal justice system, even though modified to take account of their age and understanding. We now consider the evolution of juvenile justice systems, the arguments for the welfare and justice approaches and the causes and other aspects of delinquent behaviour.

DEVELOPMENT OF A SEPARATE SYSTEM FOR JUVENILES

5.2 For most of the 20th Century juvenile offenders have enjoyed a special status under the criminal law. They are, for example, in England and Wales and in Northern Ireland, dealt with in the main by a separate juvenile court. Under the Children Act 1908, magistrates' courts dealing with juveniles under 16 were required to deal with them separately from other business, by sitting at a different place or different time. The court's jurisdiction was both civil and criminal, embracing both children in need of care and protection and those who infringed the criminal law. The Act confirmed the age of criminal responsibility as seven years of age and, on a finding of guilt, allowed courts the option of a range of custodial and non-custodial sentences, some more penal than others, designed to educate and reform rather than punish. The Act was a logical sequel to a series of reformative measures, aimed at the protection of juvenile offenders and their segregation from adult criminals, which had started in 1838 with the passing of the Parkhurst Act(which created a separate penitentiary for juvenile offenders) and included the Young Offenders Act 1901 (which required the attendance of parents in court and gave courts additional and less rigorous options as to the place of remand or committal in juvenile cases), the Probation of Offenders Act 1907 and the Prevention of Crime Act 1908 (which introduced the sentence of borstal training for offenders aged 16–21 years of age). However, whilst the Children Act 1908 mitigated the harsher elements of judicial practice as applied to children, its purpose was limited in that it did not seek to lessen a child's liability under the law: it simply provided for a separate and more sympathetic application of the law to juveniles and endorsed the belief that juveniles could normally be dealt with effectively if subjected to care and training rather than anything more punitive.

5.3 The United Kingdom was not the first country to introduce the juvenile court. In the United States of America the separate trial of adult and juvenile offenders was introduced on a regular basis in a number of states from 1870 onwards. This was followed in 1899 by the establishment in Cooke County, Illinois, of what is generally regarded as the first modern juvenile court which embraced within its jurisdiction cases of delinquency, dependency and abuse. Within 25 years all but two states in America had made legislative provision for a juvenile court on the lines of that pioneered by Illinois, though in practice the quality of provision varied greatly.

---

47. Paragraph 20.

5.4 Whilst the pressure for change in the juvenile justice field both in the United Kingdom and in America came from essentially similar sources and possibly from the same motives, the outcome in each jurisdiction was markedly different. The juvenile court in the United Kingdom, when it finally came, was firmly located within the judicial tradition of the country whereas in America the procedural characteristics of the court were seen more as a framework within which a primarily welfare orientated approach to juvenile offenders could be given expression. The Illinois Juvenile Court Act of 1899 endorsed the view that children should not be treated as criminals, that welfare considerations were paramount and that a full understanding of the child's background and circumstances was necessary and more important than the question of guilt or innocence. All court procedures and practices were to be geared to the investigation, diagnosis and treatment of the problems of the child.

5.5 By contrast, Norway in 1896, Sweden in 1902 and Denmark in 1905, in major reviews of the juvenile justice arrangements, excluded children from the criminal courts by raising the age of criminal responsibility to 14 (Norway) and 15 (Sweden and Denmark) respectively. Children below that age who committed offences were regarded as children in need of care, to be dealt with by welfare tribunals known as "child welfare panels". The panels were non-judicial in character and were conceived to educate and otherwise meet the needs of neglected children, including offenders, rather than to punish. Those offenders who were held criminally responsible, i.e. those over age 14/15, were still to be subject to prosecution unless referred to a panel by the public prosecutor. Current arrangements in Scandinavia still adhere to these original concepts.

5.6 Thus, whilst the Children Act 1908 was a legislative milestone in the treatment of young offenders in the United Kingdom it was by no means unique or particularly radical. Further refinements followed. In 1920 the Juvenile Courts (Metropolis) Act, which was restricted to London, provided for the appointment of specialist magistrates supported by lay justices in the metropolitan courts dealing with juveniles. This practice was then endorsed by the Departmental Committee on the Treatment of Young Offenders in 1927[48], subsequently adopted nationally in Great Britain by the 1932 Children and Young Persons Act and consolidated in the 1933 Act of the same name. Anticipating later developments, the Departmental Committee of 1927 also observed that there was little distinction between neglected and delinquent children and advocated greater attention be paid to the welfare requirements of children, including offenders, coming before the juvenile courts. This suggestion was subsequently adopted by the 1933 Act which included a statutory declaration to that effect. That Act also raised the age of criminal responsibility in Great Britain to eight years; required local authorities to provide remand homes to replace places of detention provided by the police under the 1908 Act; and reconstituted reformatory and industrial schools as approved schools. There was no attempt to change the juvenile court as a forum for compulsory intervention, the Departmental Committee of 1927 having supported its retention, albeit with some modification in approach, to cater for welfare considerations.

---

48. Cmnd 2381. 1927.

5.7 The Criminal Justice Act 1948 in Great Britain further restricted the imprisonment of young offenders and made provision for the establishment of attendance and detention centres. The next major development in the field of children's legislation in Great Britain, apart from the Children Act 1948 which was concerned primarily with children in care, was the Children and Young Persons Act 1963. That Act, which applied only to England and Wales, had been preceded in 1960 by the Ingleby Report[49] which emphasised the role of the family and the child's wider environment in the causality of delinquency and advocated vigorous preventive measures, with local authorities taking a central role. The Report also reflected the dilemma of juvenile courts considering a case on one ground—the commission of an offence—and disposing of it under the wider criteria of the needs of the child. The Committee, however, saw the juvenile court as offering the best safeguard to the rights and liberties of children and their parents and attempted to avoid the dilemma by recommending that the age of criminal responsibility be raised to 14, children under that age who offended being made the subject of care, protection or control proceedings rather than criminal proceedings. The Children and Young Persons Act 1963, however, only raised the age of criminal responsibility to ten years of age.

5.8 The 1963 Act was rapidly followed in England and Wales by the White Paper "The Child, the Family and the Young Offender"[50], which owed much to the Longford Report "Crime—A Challenge to us All" and advocated increasing the age of criminal responsibility to 16, the abolition of juvenile courts and the establishment of family councils comprised of social workers and other suitably experienced people to deal with all undisputed cases involving children (offenders and non-offenders) aged under 16, according to their needs. Cases of dispute would go to family courts and offenders aged over 16 would be dealt with in young offenders courts operating conventional legal procedures. Such was the opposition to these proposals, primarily from those closely associated with the juvenile court who were concerned at the possible erosion of safeguards for children, that they were soon replaced by those of the further White Paper "Children in Trouble"[51], which advocated the retention of the juvenile court within certain limitations. Magistrates were still to have charge over the determination of guilt or innocence but were no longer to be involved in detailed decisions as to treatment. This is the position under the current legislative provision in England and Wales, the Children and Young Persons Act 1969.

5.9 In Scotland legislative provision affecting juvenile offenders up to the 1960's broadly paralleled that in England and Wales. However the establishment of specialist juvenile courts of summary jurisdiction, akin to those in England and Wales, was discretionary and did not receive universal support in Scotland. Thus, whilst the legislative intent throughout Great Britain was broadly uniform, practice was not and the divergence between Scotland and England and Wales became more marked in the 1960's. The Ingleby Report did not apply to Scotland and in 1961 the Secretary of State for Scotland appointed a committee to consider existing Scottish practice, particularly the constitution, powers and procedures of the courts regarding

49. Cmnd 1191. 1960.
50. Cmnd 2472. 1965.
51. Cmnd 3601. 1968.

juvenile offenders and those in need of care, protection or control. This was the Kilbrandon Committee which, in its Report[52] of 1964, gave priority to welfare considerations in dealing with all juveniles, including offenders, as compared with those traditionally associated with courts of law. The Committee's Report, and the subsequent Social Work (Scotland) Act 1968, accepted the hypothesis that the legal classification which distinguishes children and young persons as offenders or non-offenders often belies a basic similarity of need and that the system as it then existed in Scotland was incapable of identifying and meeting these needs. The Social Work (Scotland) Act 1968, therefore, replaced the juvenile jurisdiction of Scottish courts in respect of care cases, and all but the most serious criminal cases, with a more informal and specialised welfare orientated system known as children's hearings. Details of the Scottish system including the role of the reporter, the children's panel and the sheriff court are contained in Appendix III of our Consultative Document.

5.10 In Northern Ireland the Children Act 1908 continued in force until 1950. The only legislative provision of note affecting juvenile offenders in the intervening period was the Children (Juvenile Courts) Act (Northern Ireland) 1942, which provided for two lay persons known as children's guardians to sit with the resident magistrate in cases involving juveniles. The guardians' role was limited to questioning persons giving evidence.

5.11 The Children and Young Persons Act (Northern Ireland) 1950 was based on a White Paper "Protection and Welfare of the Young and the Treatment of the Young Offender"[53], issued in 1948. The White Paper took account of developments in Great Britain since the 1908 Act and of the recommendations of the Lynn Committee which reviewed legislation affecting children in Northern Ireland and whose Report in 1938 had been shelved on the outbreak of the war. The 1950 Act replicated the welfare considerations of the 1933 Act in Great Britain; raised the age of criminal responsibility to eight years; replaced the juvenile guardians in the juvenile court with lay representatives having special experience of children and gave them equal voting rights with the presiding magistrate. The Act also included provision to prohibit publication of the identity of any child before the juvenile court and to establish training schools as a major facility available to the juvenile court.

5.12 There was no further change in Northern Ireland until the 1950 Act was replaced by the Children and Young Persons Act (Northern Ireland) 1968. This Act was largely a re-enactment of the 1950 provisions, together with such of the Ingleby recommendations as had been included in the 1963 Children and Young Persons Act in England and Wales. There was no substantial change in the basic principles upon which the 1950 Act was founded. The 1968 Act contained no hint of the more radical ideas of the mid-1960's for dealing with children and young people as presented in the Kilbrandon Report, the White Paper "The Child, The Family and the Young Offender" or of the more limited proposals of the 1968 White Paper in England and Wales "Children in Trouble". The age of criminal responsibility was raised to ten years, provision was made for the establishment of attendance centres and, perhaps the most significant change, the Act provided for closer co-operation between police and welfare authorities in deciding whether to prosecute and for the promotion of a

---

52. Children and Young Persons—Scotland. Cmnd 2306. 1964.
53. Cmnd 264. 1948.

child's welfare through the introduction of new preventive powers. The role and power of the juvenile court in dealing with juvenile offenders was preserved. This then is the position currently applying in Northern Ireland.

WELFARE OR JUSTICE

5.13 Current arrangements for dealing with juvenile offenders in the United Kingdom, and elsewhere for that matter, are the result of an accommodation of differing ideologies. Neither Scotland, nor England and Wales, nor Northern Ireland adheres rigidly to solely welfare or criminal justice principles. In Scotland welfare principles predominate but prosecution is still possible in certain circumstances. England and Wales, whilst endorsing much the same principles as Scotland, has maintained the juvenile court. So far, Northern Ireland has held more closely to the traditional tenets of the criminal law but the welfare of the child is not neglected, and indeed section 48 of the 1968 Act enunciates the principle that every court, in dealing with a juvenile, must have regard to his welfare.

5.14 The terms "welfare" and "justice" are used to describe the separate philosophies upon which particular approaches to delinquency are based. We must look beyond such generalities to the values or premises implicit in existing or new arrangements for dealing with juvenile offenders and ask ourselves whether they are reasonable, well-founded and generally in accord with the standards and expectations of the community which the system purports to serve. The evidence submitted to us simplified this task. Generally speaking there was, on the one hand, a renewed call for the extension to Northern Ireland of a more explicit welfare approach to juvenile offenders, possibly along similar lines to that in effect in Scotland, and on the other hand a continued endorsement of the criminal justice principles already evident to some extent in the existing Northern Ireland arrangements. Conceptually these are not new ideas but they have crystallised in the course of discussion both before and since the introduction of the Social Work (Scotland) Act 1968 and the Children and Young Persons Act 1969 and there is merit in setting out in detail the bases of their claims for endorsement.

5.15 The following arguments have been put forward from time to time in support of a welfare model for dealing with juvenile offenders:—

(a) delinquent, dependant and neglected children are all products of an adverse environment which at its worst is characterised by multiple deprivation. Social, economic and physical disadvantage, including poor parental care, are all relevant considerations;

(b) delinquency is a pathological condition; a presenting symptom of some deeper maladjustment out of the control of the individual concerned;

(c) since a person has no control over the multiplicity of causal factors dictating his delinquency he cannot be considered responsible for his actions or held accountable for them. Considerations of guilt or innocence are, therefore, irrelevant and punishment is not only inappropriate but is contrary to the rules of natural justice;

(d) all children in trouble (both offenders and non-offenders) are basically the same and can be effectively dealt with through a single unified system designed to identify and meet the needs of children;

(e) the needs or underlying disorders, of which delinquency is symptomatic, are capable of identification and hence treatment and control are possible;

32

(f) informality is necessary if the child's needs are to be accurately determined and his best interests served. Strict rules of procedure or standards of proof not only hinder the identification of need but are unnecessary in proceedings conducted in the child's best interests;

(g) inasmuch as need is highly individualised, flexibility of response is vital. Wide discretion is necessary in the determination and variation of treatment measures;

(h) voluntary treatment is possible and is not punishment. Treatment has no harmful side effects;

(i) the child and his welfare are paramount though considerations of public protection cannot be ignored. In any event, a system designed to meet the needs of the child will in turn protect the community and serve the best interests of society;

(j) prevention of neglect and alleviation of disadvantage will lead to prevention of delinquency.

5.16 In essence it is argued that a welfare system more adequately acknowledges the realities of life as they affect the majority of children who offend since it does not distinguish between the neglected child and the delinquent child—both are children in need who have been shaped by an environment over which they have no control. In such circumstances the concept of guilt is no longer valid. What is required is assessment, diagnosis and treatment. Procedural arrangements must be such as will facilitate the identification of individual needs and maximise the prospect of successful intervention. Flexibility is the key note. Not only are traditional legal concepts and proceedings unduly restrictive where considerations of welfare are paramount, they are largely unnecessary in the vast majority of cases involving juveniles since the facts are not generally in dispute and no question of proof of guilt arises. The real problem is in deciding how best to deal with the child or young offender involved. Here a welfare system is seen as less stigmatic— affording the individual concerned some dignity and self-respect and not confirming offenders in their anti-social behaviour by labelling them delinquent. Moreover, it is thought to provide a more intelligible forum in which both the child and his parents can discuss their problems freely and to better accommodate the attempts of professionally-qualified experts to determine the assistance and treatment required.

5.17 On the other hand, the premises which underlie the justice model are as follows:—

(a) delinquency per se is a matter of opportunity and choice—other factors may combine to bring a child to the point of delinquency but, unless there is evidence to the contrary, the act as such is a manifestation of the rational decision to that effect;

(b) insofar as a person is responsible for his actions he should also be accountable. This is qualified in respect of children by the doctrine of criminal responsibility as originally evolved under common law and now endorsed by statute. Children under the age of ten are conclusively presumed not to have the capacity to distinguish the wrongness of an act constituting an offence for which they could be punished and hence are excluded from the criminal law. Children aged 10–14 have a more limited exclusion insofar as the presumption can be rebutted on evidence that the child knew he was doing wrong;

(c) proof of commission of an offence should be the sole justification for intervention and the sole basis of punishment;

(d) society has the right to re-assert the norms and standards of behaviour endorsed by society as vital to communal living and, within reason, to constrain those whose behaviour conflicts with those standards;

(e) sanctions and controls are valid responses to deviant behaviour both as an expression of society's disapproval and as an individual and general deterrent to future similar behaviour;

(f) behaviour attracting legal intervention and associated sanctions available under the law should be specifically defined to avoid uncertainty;

(g) the power to interfere with a person's freedom and in particular that of a child should be subject to the most rigorous standard of proof which traditionally is found in a court of law. Individual rights are most effectively safeguarded under the judicial process;

(h) there should be equality before the law: like cases should be treated alike;

(i) there should be proportionality between the seriousness of the delinquent or criminal behaviour warranting intervention and the community's response; between the offence and the sentence given.

5.18 Proponents of a justice model for dealing with children who offend endorse those principles traditionally associated with the criminal law: free-will, individual responsibility and hence accountability, punishment as a valid response to influence behaviour and like penalties for like offences. It is seen as most adequately reflecting the gravity of delinquent behaviour and as underpinning the structure of society, first by denouncing criminal behaviour and second, and more indirectly, by preserving the rule of law and reinforcing the concepts of justice and fairness. It balances the rights and liberties of the individual with those of society. Concepts such as public safety and deterrents are constrained in practice by procedural safeguards for offenders, fairness between individuals and other mitigating and humanitarian considerations guaranteed by custom, tradition, natural justice and legislation.

5.19 The merit or otherwise of a particular approach to juvenile delinquency is a matter of opinion. Those who submitted views to us were clearly sincere in their belief that children and the community would be best served by endorsement of the arrangement which they advocated. Not surprisingly, however, counter-claims are made about the respective views. We will touch on these in turn.

5.20 There is, for example, a view that the welfare model is ill-conceived: that the medical analogy implicit in the welfare model over-simplifies the complexity of delinquent behaviour and its amenability to correction through welfare response. It is also said that the welfare approach is contradictory and misleading since it purports to offer help but is concerned with ensuring conformity with societal norms of behaviour and hence with effecting social control, albeit by a supposedly less painful process than might otherwise be the case. The welfare model has also been represented as being incapable of coping with serious and persistent delinquency thereby exposing the community to risk and contributing to the erosion of norms and standards endorsed by the community, as encouraging the abuse of individual rights and liberties in pursuit of what is thought to be the child's best interests and as paying insufficient regard to children who offend deliberately, regardless of the circumstances which gave rise to the inclination or opportunity to do so.

5.21 Criticism is also levelled against the justice model. Perhaps the major criticism is that implied by an acceptance of the social welfare approach: that children are brought to delinquency through disadvantage over which they have no control and that the primary aim in dealing with children in trouble should be the promotion of their welfare. In the vast majority of cases involving juvenile offenders the facts are not in dispute and hence the judicial process is largely redundant in such cases. The real problem is in deciding how best to deal with the child involved and consideration of a specific criminal act may relegate other possible important needs of the child to the secondary position. In addition, it is said that court proceedings are too formal and are often unintelligible to children and their parents, and that involvement in judicial proceedings is stigmatic and possibly destructive, often confirming children in their delinquent activities.

5.22 The welfare and justice models are both exaggerated and artificial. As we have pointed out, neither exists in the real world but they serve a useful purpose as academic models, enabling us to illustrate certain concepts and develop certain points. We do not, therefore, intend to pronounce in favour of one model and reject the other. Instead, we set out principles derived from them which we believe should be taken into account in determining how we should deal with children who break the law. We then apply these principles in considering whether our current arrangements should continue or whether any other way forward will offer a better prospect of responding in a helpful manner to children's needs and at the same time meeting society's legitimate demand for protection.

5.23 We take the view that a strategy for dealing with children who break the law must take account of the following factors:—

(a) the complexity of the factors which cause delinquency;

(b) the ubiquity of delinquency within society;

(c) the minor and transient nature of most delinquent activity;

(d) the stigmatic and possibly deleterious effects of prosecution and conviction;

(e) the widespread anxiety felt about serious and persistent offenders;

(f) the desirability, so far as possible, of dealing with young offenders in the community rather than in custody.

It must also clarify how far treatment, in the form of help or support, is considered to be an adequate response to delinquent behaviour, particularly where this has reached serious or persistent proportions. We will deal with each of these matters in turn.

The Causation of Delinquency

5.24 While some theories of delinquency assert that offenders behave as they do because of the physical or mental constitution with which they were born, most explanations suggest that delinquency arises from the interaction between an individual and his social environment. The economic, environmental and social conditions in which the delinquent develops all play a part. This was the view endorsed by the President's Commission on Law Enforcement and Administration of Justice in the United States in its report in 1967 "Juvenile Delinquency and Youth Crime"[54] which, after attributing the ineffectiveness of

---

54. US Government Printing Office. Washington D.C. 20402.

the US juvenile court to, among other things, ". . . a grossly overoptimistic view of what is known about the phenomenon of juvenile criminality . . ." said that "Study and research tend increasingly to support the view that delinquency is not so much an act of individual deviancy as a pattern of behaviour produced by a multitude of pervasive societal influences . . .". A somewhat similar understanding was evident in the 1968 White Paper "Children in Trouble" which represented delinquency as having "no single cure" but being influenced by "genetic, emotional and intellectual factors, . . . maturity, and . . . family, school, neighbourhood and . . . wider social setting . . . Sometimes it is the response to unsatisfactory family or social circumstances, a result of boredom in and out of school, an indication of maladjustment or immaturity, or a symptom of a deviant, damaged or abnormal personality".

5.25 Understanding of the causes of delinquency has not changed markedly since 1968. The White Paper on the Children and Young Persons Act 1969[55] attributed delinquency and general juvenile misbehaviour to "underlying personal, social and environmental factors" which were both "complex" and "deep rooted". It singled out a number of aspects of social and economic policy considered important in determining a young person's adjustment to the demands of society: "the quality of parental care; the support which society gives financially and in other ways to parents; the kind of housing available for families, especially in our inner urban areas, and the environment in which it is set; educational provision; recreational and other leisure facilities; the job opportunities available to young people, especially those who leave school early and with few skills". We have already noted the impact of these factors on the family generally and we have no reason to depart from the general consensus that they, together with the personal characteristics of the individual concerned, are among the multiplicity of factors which play a part in the aetiology of delinquency.

The Ubiquity of Delinquency

5.26 As stated in the White Paper, "Children in Trouble" "it is probably a minority of children who grow up without ever misbehaving in ways which may be contrary to the law . . . frequently such behaviour is no more than an incident in the pattern of a child's normal development". The ubiquity of the factors influencing juvenile behaviour discussed in paragraph 5.25 would suggest that this was the case and self-report studies of delinquency confirm this. Misbehaviour which at times might contravene the criminal law is widely recognised as typical of the adolescent experience—part and parcel of growing up. It must, however, be recognised that whilst delinquency is common among children and young people as a class, in the sense that at some time or other most young people act in a way contrary to the law, it is also generally exceptional on an individual basis, for most young people do not habitually offend. This, of course, does not make delinquency any more palatable or acceptable though it may affect our attitude to those who are apprehended and charged with a criminal offence. It points to the necessity, when dealing with young "offenders", to distinguish between the individual who has committed an isolated offence and those who habitually behave in an unacceptable manner.

---

55. Cmnd 6494. 1976.

The Nature of Juvenile Delinquency

5.27 Most juvenile offences are trivial. In England and Wales, where a substantial number of juvenile offenders are simply cautioned, the White Paper on the Children and Young Persons Act 1969 took the view that serious and persistent offenders were "a small minority among delinquent children". In Scotland the majority of juvenile offenders are not thought to merit anything more than a warning either from the police or the reporter, or some other informal, in the sense of non-compulsory, response by the reporter. Prosecution, or even compulsory intervention by a children's hearing, occurs only in a minority of cases. Whilst the pattern of detected juvenile crime in Northern Ireland differs from that in the rest of the United Kingdom (Northern Ireland has a greater proportion of robberies and crimes of malicious damage and less theft) the fact remains that the bulk of juvenile crime is still relatively minor. In recent years about 30% of juveniles dealt with by the police in Northern Ireland were cautioned rather than prosecuted and, of those prosecuted, a considerable proportion, over the whole range of offences, were given an absolute or conditional discharge. This would suggest misconduct which was not particularly grave but rather more of a nuisance than a serious source of harm to the community and certainly not sufficient to cause society to feel imperilled.

5.28 Fortunately for the community the minor nature of most juvenile crime is matched by its transience. We have already seen that most children and young people contravene the law in some way as they grow up. Many never come into contact with the police or other agencies. Most, however, do not persist in crime. Likewise, as far as we can tell, only a minority among juveniles who are prosecuted persist beyond a first or second offence. The indications are that many juvenile offenders, detected and undetected, mature out of their delinquency.

The Deleterious Effects of Prosecution and Conviction

5.29 In dealing with crime, the process of prosecution and conviction are safeguards against arbitrary action by the State, but can also have adverse consequences, particularly where children are concerned. Whatever benefits might be derived from the sentence of the court, a court appearance even for an adult is widely regarded as a destructive and stigmatic experience. For some, primarily those who have not previously been involved in criminal proceedings, the stigma attached to a court appearance may have a deterrent effect. For some children who are convicted, the experience, far from being beneficial or constructive, is often a significant step in their delinquent career, confirming them in, rather than turning them from, further delinquent activity. Once labelled a delinquent, a child is more likely to see himself as such, to associate with kindred spirits, to be a focus of attention for the police, to become stereotyped. It is now widely accepted that conviction can have the effect of increasing, rather than diminishing, juvenile criminality.

Serious and Persistent Offenders

5.30 Whilst most juvenile delinquency is of a minor and passing nature, some clearly is not. There are some children whose offences can only be construed as serious and a danger to society. So too, there are some who so persist in delinquent activity, even of a comparatively trivial nature, that their behaviour becomes intolerable. Together they are a small but troublesome minority and a source of real concern to the community. Here in Northern Ireland, as much and possibly more so than anywhere else in the United Kingdom, "there is a strongly felt and understandable demand for the public to be protected from serious and persistent, albeit youthful offenders"[56]. People expect to be safeguarded from the depredations of those who break the law, even if they are only children, and the State has a responsibility to provide protection for its citizens, if necessary by removing a child from the community for a period.

In Custody or in the Community

5.31 Over the past ten years there has been increasing emphasis on non-custodial sentences for offenders. This is reflected in the adult field in Great Britain and to a lesser degree in Northern Ireland, by such developments as parole, suspended sentences, community service orders, day training, deferment of sentence, the use of hostels both before and after conviction, and restriction on the use of imprisonment for young offenders and those who have not previously served a prison sentence. The reluctance to respond to crime simply by committing people to custody is even more evident where juveniles are concerned, and rightly so. In the wake of intermediate treatment philosophy which, though given statutory expression only in England and Wales[57], is now common throughout the United Kingdom, a wide variety of community-based programmes have been developed which seek to help juveniles who are delinquent or who are thought to run the risk of involvement in delinquent activity. Certainly among many of those engaged in dealing with juvenile offenders, if not among the community at large, the view prevails that committal to custody is to be avoided if at all possible.

5.32 There are a number of reasons for this major shift towards non-residential provision for offenders. Factors which have contributed include increasing awareness of the harmful effects of residential care; disillusionment with the results of institutional disposals in curtailing delinquency; the rising and increasingly prohibitive costs involved in residential care; and recognition that problems arising in the community, if they are to be resolved rather than simply deferred for a period, must also be tackled within the community. Even proponents of an essentially non-custodial approach to delinquents would agree that in some instances custody is unavoidable, for example, where the potential threat to the community is too great. In the words of the Eleventh Report from the Expenditure Committee on the 1969 Act[58] we must differentiate between ". . . children who need care, welfare, better education and more support from society and the small minority who need strict control and an element of punishment".

TREATMENT

5.33 We now turn to the question of whether or not treatment is a valid or adequate response to juvenile criminality. To answer this we have looked at the basis of our intervention in the lives of juvenile offenders and at the available evidence on the effects of treatment programmes for such children.

---

56. Cmnd 6494. 1976. Paragraph 4.
57. See Paragraph 3.32.
58. HMSO 534–1. 1975.

5.34 State intervention in the lives of children and young people who offend, though of late expressed in the provision of help and support rather than punishment, is motivated not simply by a desire to help the child or young person concerned but also by a desire to ensure that society is protected and that its standards of behaviour, as reflected in the criminal law, are preserved. Intervention, or even the threat of intervention, demonstrates that society is not prepared to allow its standards to be violated with impunity. It also affords the opportunity to persuade the person concerned away from further delinquency. In the past this was pursued through the imposition of constraints or punishment but more recently by seeking to influence factors considered to contribute to a child's criminality.

5.35 Though there may be reservations about the efficacy of treatment as a response to delinquency, this is not to say that children who offend do not have problems or needs, the alleviation of which would enhance their quality of life and expand their horizons to such a degree that delinquency would no longer attract them. Their needs are unlikely to differ markedly from many children who have not come into contact with the law. Consequently it might be said that children in need of care and those who offend share the same problems, but children charged with a criminal offence differ in one important respect from those who come to attention simply through obvious need, abuse or deprivation—they have by their actions come into conflict with society and society claims the right to exercise reasonable restraint over those who offend against it.

SUMMARY

5.36 To summarise therefore:—

(1) juvenile offenders have problems common to all children and like other children in need of care or assistance should have these met on their merits;

(2) most delinquency is of a minor and limited nature. Serious and persistent offences are in the minority;

(3) the impact of "treatment" on delinquency is uncertain though it may benefit a child in other ways;

(4) prosecution and conviction can have a counter-productive labelling effect and consequently should be avoided so far as is compatible with the protection of the public and the rights of the offender;

(5) intervention in the lives of offenders is dictated by the demand of society for protection as much as by a desire simply to afford help and support for those in need. Society expects protection from those who offend against it, including children. This is particularly so where their behaviour is either serious or persistent.

5.37 These are, for us, key considerations which must find expression in any policy for dealing with children who offend. We do not consider that children who commit offences should be dealt with by the same method as children in need of care. Although it is not possible to demonstrate conclusively that any age is particularly appropriate for knowledge of right and wrong, we accept the assumptions relating to the age of criminal responsibility set out in paragraph 5.17(b). Accordingly, we would not wish to recommend any change in the age of criminal responsibility.

5.38 We consider that the interests of all concerned, including those of juveniles themselves, would be best served by the pursuit of a strategy designed to identify and counter disadvantage and need at an early stage and by the clear assertion of acceptable standards of behaviour, initially in an informal and supportive fashion and subsequently by a judicially-based system. We seek, therefore, a realistic balance between welfare and justice.

6—The Control of Delinquent Behaviour

6.1 In proposing[59] that juvenile offenders[60] should continue to be dealt with within the criminal justice system, we draw an important distinction between, on the one hand, infrequent minor offences and, on the other, persistent or serious offences.

MINOR OFFENDERS

6.2 At present many children whose behaviour, though technically a criminal offence, is considered more of a nuisance than a serious source of harm to the community, are given a word of advice rather than an official caution or prosecution and we expect this practice to continue. If the offence is of more consequence, but still not serious, the child may be cautioned formally. About one-third of juvenile offenders dealt with by the police in Northern Ireland are cautioned in contrast to the 46% cautioned in England and Wales in 1977. This does not mean that those appearing before the courts in Northern Ireland are a hard core of offenders because, in addition to the proportion given an absolute or conditional discharge (around 36% in 1977), a further 30% are fined. It is unlikely that so many would be allowed to remain in the community if their offences were sufficiently serious to cause alarm. We consider that there is, therefore, room for a substantial extension of police cautioning.

6.3 Cautioning accords with the principle that intervention by the State in the life of an individual following the commission of an offence should be the minimum possible commensurate with the protection of the public. As most children who offend admit guilt, it is often an unnecessary waste of resources to proceed to prosecution and a finding of guilt. We recognise, however, that any alternative must ensure that the child's rights are adequately safeguarded. Whilst cautioning reinforces and maintains the standards of behaviour endorsed by the majority of society, it affords a framework within which children who might have problems can receive help whilst remaining within their own families and community.

6.4 We envisage an extension of the present juvenile liaison scheme so that all first and second minor offenders who admit guilt should be cautioned by the police. The child would be warned formally by the police, in the presence of his parents, of the consequences of continued delinquent behaviour. The police would advise the parents, where necessary, of possible sources of assistance in coping with the child or other family problems. The acceptance of help would be voluntary. In any event the existing practice would continue whereby there is a statutory[61] duty upon the police to inform the local social services department when a formal caution has been administered. The police should also inform the school principal of the caution.

6.5 Only cases which pose a real or serious threat to society would go before the juvenile court: society is unlikely to accept perpetual warning of minor offenders who persist in delinquent activity. Prosecution would be the normal

---

59. Paragraph 5.38.
60. In this chapter references to offenders are to children aged ten years and over but under the age of 17.
61. Section 163 Children and Young Persons Act (Northern Ireland) 1968.

procedure after a second caution and the offender's previous cautions should continue to be referred to in court as an indication of his involvement in delinquent activity. This should be made clear to the child and his parents as part of the cautioning procedure. It is envisaged that the life of a caution for referral to in court should be limited to three years.

6.6 We recognise there may be problems in defining what constitutes a minor offence. There are guidelines available using, for example, the offences already defined by the police as minor under the existing cautioning arrangements. Serious offences would certainly include murder, attempted murder, firearms offences, explosives offences, a number of offences against the person and robbery. However, the determination of offences as minor or serious needs further consideration and we recommend that the police, judiciary and the legal profession should be asked for their views.

6.7 There are other practical issues which require comment in connection with cautioning:—

(i) *Form and standard of proof*

Cautions would be administered only to those young persons who admit the offence. To avoid the accusation that innocent children will plead guilty to "get off lightly", the current RUC practice of proceeding with the investigation up to the point where there is sufficient evidence to support a prosecution should continue to be carried out before the cautioning process is embarked upon.

(ii) *Procedural safeguards*

Children should be interviewed where possible in the presence of a parent/guardian or other adult friend, and the interview should take place at a location which does not intimidate or embarrass the child or young person. Enquiries concerning the parents or guardians should, as far as possible, be confined to the home.

(iii) *Rights and attitudes of the victim*

The extension of cautioning may disadvantage victims to some extent by removing the prospect of compensation awarded by the court had the case gone to hearing. Any such loss—and against this the likelihood or otherwise of the offender or his parents being in a position to pay compensation—should be taken into account when a caution is being considered. However, the views of the victim should not be conclusive since the option of a private prosecution[62] will still be available.

(iv) *Multiple offences*

Problems may arise when a child, coming into contact with the police for the first time, is connected with a series of previous offences or several offences arising out of a single criminal incident. A low-level response may give a criminally experienced young person a distorted view not only of the criminal justice system but also of the community's attitude to his and other criminal activity. Each case would have to be dealt with on its merits.

---

62. Prosecution of Offences (Northern Ireland) Order 1972, Article 5(3).

6.8 Since our proposals for diversion from the courts through cautioning are an extension of the current RUC juvenile liaison scheme, the mechanics should remain essentially the same. Where the guilt of a child has been admitted, his case should be passed to a juvenile liaison officer who would be concerned with gathering the outstanding information required by the criteria governing cautioning. The case would then be reviewed by a police officer, of not less than Chief Inspector rank, who would decide whether to caution or prosecute. When a caution is opted for, an Inspector in uniform would warn the offender, in the presence of parents or guardians and the juvenile liaison officer, of the consequences of future misconduct. The caution should be followed by a period of regular contact between the young person, his parents or guardians and the juvenile liaison officer, the primary purpose of which would be to assist the parents or guardians and keep the child from further infringement of the law.

6.9 When there is evidence justifying prosecution for an offence, the criteria to be used in considering whether a caution would be more appropriate might include:—

the seriousness of the alleged offence, the circumstances in which the offence was allegedly committed, and the length of time that had passed since the alleged occurrence;

the danger to the public represented by the child and the possibility of the repetition of the offence, or of similar, or other, offences;

the previous history of the child; and

any plans put forward by or on behalf of the child to make amends.

6.10 Under our proposals many of the children who come to the attention of the police may have been identified as children in need and may already be known to agencies represented on School-based Care Teams recommended in Chapter 3. This will again be an extension of the current scheme in which juvenile liaison officers take an interest in children in need. We envisage that, after a caution has been administered, additional support from social and educational agencies should be directed towards those children already identified. Where the child has not been previously established as in need, the local social services department would be informed and, in addition, the school-based team would be informed, where it is thought they could help. Diversion from the criminal justice system will therefore be part of a strategy which envisages co-ordinated action to meet need and disadvantage generally. Acceptance of the help offered to the child and his parents by these agencies would be voluntary.

6.11 As we see it diversion is not a soft option: rather it is a positive response to delinquency, which aims to help and encourage children to channel their energy and desires into legitimate activities. We believe there are four factors contributing to this aim. First, by definition, if correctly identified, the child involved is not a persistent delinquent and might well, like many others not detected, mature out of the offending phase. Second, the police warning and supervision should have an impact on the child making him think of the consequences before reoffending. Third, the warning should alert the child's family, who may not previously have been aware of his activities or of the company he keeps. This should increase the prospect that they would exert a positive influence on him. Finally, notification to the helping agencies should result in efforts to deal with any negative factors in the child's life.

SERIOUS AND PERSISTENT OFFENDERS AND THOSE WHO DISPUTE GUILT

6.12 We accept that, despite the programme of help and diversion previously outlined, some juveniles cannot be dealt with by diversionary methods. This may be because they deny the allegation, or because they are so persistently delinquent, or their offences so serious, that a caution is inappropriate. Where guilt is at issue we share the Kilbrandon Committee's view that any departure from the due process of law is undesirable. For those cases where persistent or serious offences are to be considered, there must be adequate sanctions combined with safeguards for the rights of the individual. We suggest that only a court can meet all these requirements.

6.13 Children charged with criminal offences are (with certain well-defined exceptions) dealt with separately from adults in juvenile courts. We think this is right, but as indicated[63] we consider that the juvenile criminal court should be separate and distinct from the court dealing with care cases. In the remaining paragraphs of this chapter, in reference to "the court", we intend a juvenile court dealing only with criminal cases.

6.14 The main functions of the court would be to try offences in a manner which is fair to the defendant and easily understood by him, and to use its powers for the protection of the public and the prevention of crime.

6.15 Thus the disposals which we envisage for the court will be designed to control the child and influence his future behaviour. This does not mean that his personal or family problems should be ignored. On charging a juvenile offender, the police should refer the case to the District Child Care Team[64] and the team would ensure that help is offered by the social services department or the education agencies as appropriate.

6.16 We do not anticipate that the help or support required by children will be unduly impeded by the disposals available to the court. Most options will allow the offender to remain in the community. Even in those minority of cases involving custodial orders the provision of help or support will only be constrained by the offender's absence from his normal environment. Any help offered to the offender whilst in custody should be complemented by help to his family in an effort to resolve any problems which may have contributed to the earlier delinquent behaviour.

6.17 Inevitably cases will arise in which care considerations are so evident that immediate action is necessary to secure the welfare of the child. In these circumstances the juvenile court should be able to adjourn the case, or defer passing sentence, to allow follow-up action by the caring agencies. Where the child is charged with a serious crime, the court obviously would take account of any potential risk to the public in making its decision. If care proceedings are to

---

63. Paragraph 4.5.
64. Paragraphs 3.21–3.23.

be undertaken instead of criminal proceedings they should be justified solely on care grounds and not on the basis of the offence, which will still fall to be dealt with by the juvenile criminal court. The latter's decision, however, is likely to be influenced by the outcome of the care proceedings.

6.18 We still envisage the juvenile criminal court having access to full information about the child's history and background. Not only will this allow assessment of the degree, of culpability of the child and the likelihood of his reoffending, but it will allow the court also to determine the genuineness of an assurance by the offender or his family that they will seek assistance or attempt to solve a particular problem, the resolution of which may affect the penalty to be imposed. The court should be made aware of information which is relevant to its sentencing power, for example, there is little point in imposing a fine on a child or his parent[65] when there is unemployment or low income in the family.

6.19 Juvenile courts will wish to have reports supplied by a specialist body knowledgeable in criminal matters and experienced in dealing with offenders. We consider that the Probation Service should be the main report-providing agency. The precise content of the reports will be a matter for discussion between the juvenile courts and the Probation Service and might usefully be incorporated in a code of practice[66] for the Probation Service.

6.20 Against the background of a broad preventive strategy, co-ordinated by the District Child Care Team, the number of cases coming before a criminal court in which care considerations would come to light for the first time, or where action on care grounds would not already have begun, should be small. The District Child Care Team should, therefore, be a valuable source of information for reports to the courts, and they should liaise closely with the Probation Service. In those few cases where care considerations are clearly paramount a report should be presented to the court by the appropriate agency after consultation within the District Child Care Team. Should the team and the Probation Service disagree as to the appropriate course of action both reports should be presented to the court.

JUDICIAL OPTIONS

6.21 The court dealing with juvenile offenders must have a variety of options open to it, ranging from non-custodial measures—which allow it to admonish occasional, minor delinquent behaviour whilst leaving responsibility for future good behaviour with the child and his parents—to more restrictive powers which might be reserved for serious or persistent offenders. In addition, the power to defer passing sentence, if used discriminatingly, can provide a breathing space for offenders to come to terms with their problems.

6.22 Among the measures which are currently available to the juvenile court, and which we think should be retained, are absolute discharge, conditional discharge, binding over, fine and the award of compensation. An absolute discharge, possibly accompanied by a warning, might be imposed where the court, having found the offence proved, does not consider any sanction necessary, possibly taking the view that the offence was an isolated incident rather than an early step on the road to a delinquent career. A conditional

---

65. See section 76(1) Children and Young Persons Act (Northern Ireland) 1968.
66. Paragraph 7.6.

discharge on the other hand would indicate that, whilst the offence might be of minor significance, the court is concerned about the risk of repetition. The period of the conditional discharge should not exceed one year, and if a further offence were committed in this period the court could penalise the new offence and the original offence for which the conditional discharge was granted. Binding over is similar to the conditional discharge. It differs in as much as the young person or his parent[67] enters into an undertaking—a kind of contract for good behaviour—and knows precisely what the penalty will be if the contract is broken. The penalty is normally the forfeiture of a specified sum of money. Binding over, which is normally for a period of up to one year, can be in lieu of, or in addition to, any other penalty imposed by the court for the same offence. Whilst a fine can be imposed for all sentences except murder, it is more appropriate for less serious, and non-violent, crimes. The present provisions on parental responsibility and the present maximum amounts[68] which can be imposed should continue. This applies also to the payment of compensation by a young person or his parents for loss or damage arising out of a criminal offence. The maximum amount payable has recently been raised to £1,000. We consider the power to order payment of compensation to be particularly appropriate where the court considers it necessary to bring home to the parents their responsibility for controlling their children. In this context, we think the court might consider asking the offender to make some form of restitution to those who may have suffered from his actions.

6.23   As well as the disposals we have outlined, the juvenile court should have powers to deal with more serious or persistent delinquents. It should be able to supplement parental control with the additional authority of a supervising officer and, in the last resort, have the power partially or totally to restrict a young person's freedom of action.

6.24   Another option open to the court is to defer making an order in respect of an offender following a finding of guilt. This gives the court the opportunity to put the offender to the test regarding any promise of future good behaviour before finally making a disposal. The court might wish to defer making an order following a finding of guilt where a young offender undertakes to take advantage of help or support provided by social work departments or his school. In this way the continuing court interest in an offender's behaviour, which is characteristic of deferment, could be of value in the prevention of future delinquency. However, any undertaking entered into by the young person must be voluntary and cannot be a requirement of the court if the current deferment concept is to be followed. At the moment the responsibility for reporting an offender's conduct during his period of deferment is generally given to the Probation Service. If a child were to enter into a voluntary agreement to co-operate with the social service department, the social worker concerned would be required to report progress. The court might be slow to use deferment in those cases where the offender's behaviour clearly poses a real threat to the public but may reserve it for a more persistent, though possibly less serious, offender.

6.25   Supervision of offenders in the community is an attempt to influence their activities and life-style through the provision of help and guidance.

---

67. Section 76(2) Children and Young Persons Act (Northern Ireland) 1968.
68. Under section 72(1) of the 1968 Act these are £15 for a child and £50 for a young person.

Control is also present, in that breach of a probation order can render the offender liable to a further penalty for the original offence. The balance between help and supervision is difficult to achieve and we feel that the Probation Service needs to develop ways of ensuring that supervision is effective. The primary responsibility for the provision of whatever help or support may be necessary for the offender should however lie with the appropriate agency, e.g. in education cases with the Education and Library Board. If the court imposes a probation order the probation officer oversees the behaviour and activities of the young person for the period of the order, which should run for a maximum of one year.

6.26 Whilst in some cases parental support plus intermittent contact between an offender and his supervising officer, of the type implicit in a probation order, may prove an effective check on a young person's delinquent activity, there will be occasions when some further restriction on leisure time might be warranted. We feel that the juvenile court should continue to have a disposal similar to the present attendance centre order. We envisage that the court should be able to order a child to forego his free time and attend a juvenile centre either on an hourly basis on a Saturday or, in more serious cases where stringent restriction of leisure time appears justified, on a residential basis for a number of week-ends. In the former instance the maximum number of hours attendance might be 24 to be discharged over a six-month period: in the latter the number of days residential attendance should not be more than 15 days for children under 14 and not more than 30 days for young persons aged 14–17. Again the order might be discharged over a six-month period according to the directions of the supervising officer. The programme within such a residential centre might combine ingredients of the current attendance centre programme with schemes which might enable him to make a useful contribution to the community.

6.27 The establishment of week-end residential centres of the kind we contemplate involves a risk that children who would not otherwise be removed from home will in future be required to be away at week-ends. Notwithstanding this risk, however, we consider that giving courts the power to order week-end attendance is more desirable than simply limiting them to a residential order, the effect of which is complete removal from home. Short-term periodic attendance at a juvenile centre should not unduly disrupt a child's normal education or substantially impair his contact with his family and environment. We are therefore proposing a system which avoids, if possible, the total removal of children from their homes and the community.

6.28 At present a juvenile court has a number of custodial options open to it when dealing with an offender. It can order that the child or young person be held in a remand home up to one month, or six months for a scheduled offence. Alternatively it can impose a training school order or, if the young person has attained the age of 16, a period of borstal training. Both the training school order and a sentence of borstal training are semi-determinate. Though there is a maximum period beyond which the child or young person cannot be held, he can be discharged before that date depending on his conduct whilst in custody. Finally, for very serious offences a higher court, and in certain circumstances a juvenile court, can make an order of detention under section 73 of the Children and Young Persons Act (Northern Ireland) 1968 which may be for a fixed period or during the Secretary of State's pleasure. The place of detention is a matter for the Secretary of State.

6.29 Whilst we do not wish to alter the existing provision of section 73 of the 1968 Act, we think it desirable that the other orders should be amalgamated into a single order which would be determinate and which would attract remission. In our opinion courts should be given the opportunity, denied them under the semi-determinate training school order and borstal sentence, of fixing the period to be spent in custody in accordance with their assessment of the gravity of the offence and the potential danger to society, rather than leaving release dates to be settled by others according to different criteria. The maximum period available to the juvenile court under this new custodial order should be two years and the minimum period one month. The period in custody should attract half remission and be reduced by the time spent in custody on remand. This would ensure parity with those over age 17 given a determinate sentence and would afford a measure of control over those in custody, who could lose remission if they behaved badly.

6.30 A custodial unit for juveniles should be secure, ensuring they remain there for the period required, but it should also be as helpful and supportive as possible. Many of the principal elements of training school programmes will remain. Juveniles of compulsory school age would receive education, older children would receive vocational training and recreational and other social activities would be provided. The aim should be to provide all the normal features of a humanitarian regime consistent with the need to exercise control over those committed to custody.

6.31 In view of the limited number of girls likely to be committed to custody for serious offences it would not be practicable to provide a separate secure establishment. The custodial unit should, therefore, cater for boys and girls. It should also be non-denominational. We envisage a single establishment with a capacity of, say, 120.

6.32 It is perhaps worth restating that we expect a reduction in numbers because a custodial order should be reserved for those who are clearly a threat to society. Long-term custody should be used sparingly and only in particularly serious or harmful cases. There may be instances in which, by their persistence in crime, more minor offenders would be committed to custody, but in view of the variety of options we propose for the court we feel this should only happen in a few cases. With the introduction of the new custodial sentence and the establishment of a closed unit, the practice of transferring difficult children to borstal should cease.

TRAINING SCHOOLS

6.33 This proposal will have implications for the future of the present training schools and we now look at how the schools might be used in the future. At present there are five training schools—Rathgael, Lisnevin and St Patrick's for boys, Whiteabbey and St Joseph's for girls—and an inter-agency day unit at Whitefield House. Lisnevin Special Unit (legally a training school) with rare exceptions receives no referrals direct from the juvenile court. Its population comes from the two boys' training schools and its function is to deal with particularly difficult and disruptive children. The problems and difficulties these children face spring from a variety of causes that are not normally directly relevant to any offence they have committed.

6.34 As the two girls' training schools deal principally with non-offenders we would see them more naturally fitting into the overall preventive framework which we have outlined and becoming the responsibility of the Department of Health and Social Services. We would also see the work carried on at Lisnevin with difficult children fitting more appropriately into the preventive and care framework.

6.35 We do not see a role for two training schools of the size of St Patrick's and Rathgael, nor do we think that either of these schools would be ideal as the custodial establishment we have recommended. Both have skilled and dedicated staff and extensive facilities, and could become part of the range of residential provision required by our proposals in Chapter 4. They might also be very useful as centres for intermediate treatment.

6.36 The three functions performed by Whitefield House—the work of the Assessment Unit, the development of intermediate treatment programmes and the work of the Truancy Unit—are all activities which fall within the preventive, rather than the criminal justice, framework and, as one of our objectives has been to increase the effectiveness and scope of preventive measures, we would see these functions being absorbed into the preventive machinery.

6.37 The various non-custodial and custodial options described will give the courts sufficient powers to deal with most juvenile offenders. However, there will be some exceptional cases in which special measures are needed. We have already indicated[69] that the powers conferred by section 73 of the Children and Young Persons Act (Northern Ireland) 1968 should be retained. In addition we feel that the powers conferred by section 79 of the 1968 Act should also be retained. This section allows a juvenile court to deal summarily with an indictable offence, other than homicide, if it thinks it expedient to do so and the parents or guardian of the young person agree. The court may then make any order which might have been made if the case had been tried on indictment. Otherwise the juvenile court would simply carry out a preliminary investigation under the Magistrates' Courts Act (Northern Ireland) 1964, or a preliminary enquiry based on written documentation under the Criminal Procedure (Committal for Trial) Act (Northern Ireland) 1968 with a view, if sufficient cause is found, to returning the young offender for trial to a higher court. Also, the juvenile court should continue to have the same capacity to make a hospital or guardianship order in respect of a mentally disordered offender as it has at the moment under the Mental Health Act (Northern Ireland) 1961.

COMPOSITION OF THE COURT IN CRIMINAL PROCEEDINGS

6.38 We began by suggesting that a court dealing with juveniles should be able to establish the facts at issue, the guilt or innocence of the offender, and determine how best the public might be protected. These factors define the court as being essentially judicial in character, thus making a strong argument for legal knowledge within the court. We also see much advantage in having lay involvement in the juvenile court and we recommend that the juvenile court in criminal proceedings should continue to be comprised of a full-time legally qualified chairman (a resident magistrate) accompanied by two members drawn from a panel of lay people. The essential quality of lay involvement is in representativeness of the community at large. Within a strategy which seeks to

---

69. Paragraph 6.29.

emphasise community responsibility for the containment or control of delinquent behaviour, representation from the widest possible spectrum of society is important. Representatives of the communities from which juvenile offenders come—and therefore people who have a major interest in how such young people are dealt with—should be included. As our overall strategy places responsibility for support on the family, the school and the community, as well as the social and educational agencies, rather than on the court, lay membership should provide the court with a balanced view of society's attitude to juvenile crime and its repercussions on the community at large. To achieve this a broadly-based panel is essential.

6.39 We appreciate there may be practical difficulties in achieving the degree of representativeness we propose. At present panel members must be fairly readily available, often at short notice, and, on present rates of remuneration, reasonably self-supporting. Nevertheless, we think some improvement on the present situation is possible. In our view there is merit in the Scottish procedure of recruiting panel members through public advertisement but, if this procedure is to be followed in Northern Ireland, the application and selection process should be such as will facilitate, rather than discourage, applicants who do not have professional familiarity with documentation and interviewing—though obviously some facility in this regard will be necessary to cope with the duties of lay membership. Employers should allow members time off to attend their duties, making up any differential in pay as in other areas of the public service. At present lay members appointed to the juvenile court panel undergo training, normally taken as an extra-mural course. We consider that the lay membership should be given the opportunity to become familiar with legal concepts and the powers available to the court before full membership of the panel is ratified. The panel of lay magistrates in criminal cases should be distinct from that in care proceedings.

6.40 We have dealt at some length with our conception of the role of the lay panel in the juvenile criminal court. This is not a reflection on the present lay panel membership, who have discharged their duties in an admirable fashion and have rendered great service to the community. The changes we propose are a consequence of the new principles which we consider should govern the future operation of the juvenile criminal court.

ATMOSPHERE OF THE COURT

6.41 Whilst some formality and certain fixed procedures may be necessary to ensure that children's rights are protected, much of the effectiveness of the court will be lost if the proceedings are unintelligible to children and their parents. We should like to see all proceedings involving children conducted in a manner which is sensitive to their age and understanding, but which still affords them adequate protection of their rights.

6.42 The balance between informality, to ensure understanding, and formality to ensure protection of rights, may be difficult to strike, particularly where the professional members of the court deal with adult cases as well. We consider that this problem would be resolved best by having specialist magistrates dealing exclusively with juvenile cases and selected not only on the basis of their legal expertise but also for their interest in, and understanding of, juveniles and juvenile crime. We feel this would make it easier to achieve the ideal of having children's cases heard apart from all other cases. There may be practical difficulties involving changes in allocation of resident magistrates to districts and dates and times of court sittings, but we consider these changes should be possible without any significant reduction in the number of juvenile courts throughout Northern Ireland. Members of the court, court staff and any legal representatives coming into the juvenile court, should be expected to know the appropriate law relating to children and be able to communicate effectively with all the parties in the case.

6.43 In Northern Ireland, unlike the rest of the United Kingdom, when criminal legal aid is granted no contribution is sought from the recipient. Thus a child brought before a juvenile court will have free legal aid as a right. There is an additional safeguard in that a custodial sentence cannot be imposed unless the child is legally represented or has been given the opportunity to acquire legal representation before sentence. We are anxious, however, that when a child first becomes the subject of police enquiries the same concern should be shown for his interests and that he should have ready access to legal advice. We are encouraged, therefore, that the availability of legal aid and advice is now being publicised more widely than in the past and we hope this will continue. We should like to see more specialisation in juvenile matters by solicitors and barristers and a greater awareness of this aspect of the law by those responsible for legal education and training.

SUMMARY

6.44 To summarise, therefore:—

(1) juvenile offenders should continue to be dealt with within the criminal justice system;

(2) minor offenders should be dealt with through a police caution and the cautioning system should be extended;

(3) serious or persistent offenders should be dealt with by a juvenile court dealing solely with criminal cases;

(4) we stress the importance of the use of non-custodial disposals and suggest ways of strengthening the non-custodial disposals available to the court;

(5) there should be one custodial establishment for young offenders in Northern Ireland.

7—The Probation Service

7.1 Our terms of reference include consideration of the "future administration of the Northern Ireland Probation Service". A substantial part of the Probation Service's resources are devoted to the provision of reports on, and the subsequent supervision of, children coming before the juvenile court, primarily following the commission of an offence. Our recommendations on the wider issue of how, in future, this group of children and young people might be dealt with are, therefore, of crucial importance to the role of the Probation Service and hence also to the sort of administrative structure which might best enable the Service to discharge any new responsibilities together with its current responsibilities towards adults.

7.2 In our Consultative Document[70] we set out some of the arguments for retaining the Probation Service as a separate service and the case for the Probation Service being absorbed into the social services departments of Health and Social Services Boards. We have considered these possible courses of action and have heard evidence from a number of bodies on how the Probation Service might best discharge its responsibilities in the future. We consider that there are three options for the future management of the Service:—

(i) the Service remains a separate body responsible as at present to the Northern Ireland Office;

(ii) the Service remains a separate body responsible to a Probation Committee with membership drawn from the community;

(iii) the Service could be absorbed into the social service departments.

7.3 In setting out how the police and courts should react to young offenders we have laid stress on an increased use of non-custodial measures. To realise our objectives for juvenile offenders will not be easy. It will be necessary to provide a range of responses which can be operated within the community without undue risk to the public and which will, at the same time, restrict potential re-offending to a minimum. Our recommendations in paragraphs 6.25–6.27 are designed to this end. Their implementation, however, will require considerable skill and determination and the relationship between the Service, which will have responsibility for these disposals, the courts and the community will be crucial to the success of non-custodial disposals.

7.4 As we consider that juvenile offenders should continue to come within the criminal justice system and be dealt with when necessary by a specialist juvenile court, we do not think it appropriate that the Probation Service should become part of the general social services. We consider that the Probation Service should remain a separate service specialising in dealing with offenders and serving the criminal courts. The Service should continue to be responsible for the development and the oversight of all non-custodial disposals where supervision in different degrees is envisaged. It should have responsibility for any day-attendance or residential centres. The Service should also be the main source of social information for the criminal courts. Its aim should be to make

---

70. Consultative Document—Chapter VI.

the non-custodial disposals as effective as custody in preventing re-offending, at least for the period during which offenders are under supervision.

7.5 The Service is at present administered directly by the Northern Ireland Office and from an administrative point of view this may well be satisfactory. However, if the Service is to enjoy fully the confidence of the community, which will be essential if it is to carry out its work successfully, we consider that this can be better achieved if the community participates directly in the management of the Service. We recommend, therefore, that the Probation Service be administered by a Committee drawn from a wide spectrum of the community in Northern Ireland. This Committee will be responsible for the administration and management of the Probation Service in its expanded role. The Committee, which would be appointed by the Secretary of State, would be empowered to appoint sub-committees to look after particular aspects of the Service's work. One of these sub-committees would replace the Community Service Committee. The Northern Ireland Office should continue to be the Government Department responsible for the Probation Service and should retain financial control.

7.6 The main thrust of the Service's activities, as we see it, will be the provision of a specialist service to the courts and involvement with the community in the management of the offender. It will be important that the Chief Probation Officer and his staff bring their professional expertise to bear on the difficulties which will undoubtedly arise in carrying out the strategy we have envisaged. We have already said[71] that we consider that a written code of practice should be drawn up by the Probation Service in consultation with the Northern Ireland Courts Service and with the approval of the Secretary of State. The purpose of the code would be to ensure that the courts, the public, the probation officer and the offender were all familiar with the minimum expectations and requirements of the particular form of supervision imposed by the court. The code of practice would also apply to the Probation Service's activities with adults.

7.7 We consider that the Probation Committee should have responsibility for the management of the custodial establishment to be set up to cater for the more serious and persistent juvenile offenders. We do not think it appropriate that the juvenile custodial establishment should be part of the adult penal system. A separate committee set up specifically to run the establishment on the lines of the present training school management boards would be an obvious possibility. However, this would, in our view, mean a duplication of administrative effort and, more important, would once again place those in custody apart from the community at large, and divorce them from the general involvement which we wish to see between the community and young offenders. In our view a committee which has responsibility for all penalties for juveniles up to and including custody would bring a more balanced approach to young offenders and could help in keeping children out of custody.

---

71. Paragraph 6.19.

8—Planning and Resources

8.1 In developing our strategy we have acknowledged the contribution being made to child care in Northern Ireland by voluntary organisations. We have mentioned also the need for adequate resources to be made available if our recommendations are to be effectively implemented. We wish to reinforce the importance of these factors before summarising the main thrust of our proposals.

POLICY AND PLANNING — THE ROLE OF THE VOLUNTARY SECTOR

8.2 In our Consultative Document[72] we posed questions about the need for "an integrated system of care and treatment" and "to allocate planning and co-ordinating functions, perhaps for the whole of Northern Ireland, to a body similar in concept to regional planning committees in England and Wales". We are not, however, recommending a system of care identical to that introduced by the 1969 Act in England and Wales and, taking account of the control and responsibility already exercised by central Government Departments in Northern Ireland, we do not see a need for a highly-structured system of planning of services and facilities.

8.3 If our recommendations for a wider range of residential facilities are implemented, involving inter alia a change in use for the existing training schools, the importance of the contribution being made by voluntary organisations cannot be ignored in planning for the future. At present voluntary bodies provide over 60% of the places in residential accommodation for children; there are 24 voluntary children's homes registered under the 1968 Act as compared to 26 statutory homes. The voluntary facilities range from specialist nursery units for pre-school children to hostels for teenagers who go out to work. There are also two voluntary training schools for boys and girls.

8.4 In response to the Consultative Document some voluntary organisations saw a case for formal co-ordinating machinery. The general weight of opinion favoured some means of contributing to the formation of child care policy and plans and we accept the case for this. We consider it important for the voluntary sector to be able to make its views known on the future provision of services and facilities for children. We do not propose the establishment of any new machinery. The Central Personal Social Services Advisory Committee contains a number of representatives of voluntary and statutory child care agencies and a Standing Sub-Committee of the Central Committee should be appointed to advise the Department of Health and Social Services on all matters relating to child care. If necessary members could be co-opted to ensure comprehensive representation of both sectors.

RESOURCES

8.5 In our Introduction[73] we stressed the need for adequate resources with which to implement our recommendations. While some of our proposals will not require substantial additional expenditure, others are difficult to quantify

---

72. Paragraphs 102–104.
73. Paragraph 1.6.

but will demand some financial commitment. The emphasis on prevention will require some change in approach but we hope that the main features of our recommended strategy, including the team approach, will entail little expense. Nevertheless, if any preventive strategy is to be fully effective there must be adequate staffing levels in the various agencies, whether in social work, child health, schools, educational psychology, the education welfare service, the Probation Service or the RUC's juvenile liaison branch.

8.6 Apart from the staffing implications, the most significant expenditure is likely to be required in providing a wider range of residential facilities. Although we suggest[74] that much could be achieved by the use of peripatetic teams, there are insufficient facilities for day or residential assessment. There is a need also for adolescent centres, including accommodation for disturbed young people requiring specialised care. Against this, however, should be set any saving arising from the proposed transfer of the existing training schools to other purposes; these schools represent a very significant investment in staff as well as in premises.

8.7 While staff and accommodation may demand the greatest investment, some of our other proposals also have resource implications. These include the expansion of fostering, both on traditional lines and for difficult-to-place children; for the development of community-based schemes; and the improvement of provision for the under fives. Our emphasis on the importance of the family would also lend support to the further development of family care centres in line with current proposals by the Health and Social Services Boards in selected areas of social need.

8.8 We are aware of the need to exercise financial restraint but we consider that the provision of adequate resources for a preventive strategy could save money in the longer term.

---

74. Paragraph 4.37.

9—Summary and List of Recommendations

9.1 In preparing our Report we have taken account of the social, economic and environmental factors which have a bearing on family and child development and we have tried to set our proposals in a wider perspective. We have had to assess the possible effects of civil unrest. We have stressed the importance of reinforcing the family and the community to help children develop through the difficult period of childhood and adolescence, and avoiding the labelling of children at an early age. We take the view that such help as is needed should be provided as far as possible in the normal educational or community setting.

9.2 We accept that the best help to the developing child is a stable and secure environment with caring adults. This caring environment is most likely to be found in a well-functioning family and we are concerned to strengthen the capacity of families and communities to support their children through childhood and adolescence. In Northern Ireland, as elsewhere in the United Kingdom, communities are disintegrating and the influence of the extended family is being eroded. However, family structures are stronger here and should be utilised and strengthened.

9.3 The essential features of our strategy are prevention and co-ordination. Where problems do occur we advocate early and accurate identification and our approach is to seek support for children through the family, school and the community, requiring co-operation and communication between parents and children, between families and the community, and between the wide range of voluntary and statutory agencies which have a responsibility to help children and to prepare them for adult life. We have, therefore, recommended the establishment of teams based on selected schools and the setting up of District Child Care Teams. The team approach is aimed at ensuring better co-ordination and a comprehensive examination of the needs of each child.

9.4 Where care proceedings are considered necessary we propose that these should continue to be a matter for judicial determination. They will be dealt with by the juvenile court specialising in civil matters, although in the longer term we would wish the concept of a family court to be seriously considered. In cases requiring compulsory intervention the court will have available to it a care order and a supervision order.

9.5 While we recognise the importance of both fostering and residential care in helping individual children, we are concerned that the decision on care in each case should be related to the needs of the individual child. For this reason we are recommending that the statutory preference for fostering should be dropped. We place much emphasis on care in the community, however, and suggest that residential care should be seen as one of a range of options rather than an inevitable first choice. Children in need of care, including truants, requiring removal from home will no longer be held in the same institutions as offenders. We suggest that the needs of individual children might best be met in smaller domestic-scale residential establishments and that where there is a need for additional facilities this is more likely to be for a range of small specialised units to accommodate those children with particular needs. There will be a change in the needs which training schools were developed to meet, requiring a change of approach in these establishments. We were highly impressed, however, by the skill, devotion and dedication of staff involved in the residential care field, including the training schools, and we are confident that they will welcome the opportunity to continue to help children in new and imaginative ways in a more open system.

9.6 While all children at some stage of their development may exhibit anti-social tendencies there will only be a relatively small number who commit offences of a seriousness which society cannot tolerate or who show themselves to be persistent offenders. We have not recommended any change in the present age of criminal responsibility although we consider that minor offenders should not be prosecuted but should be dealt with through an extended use of police cautioning and, at the same time, should be given help to overcome any personal or family problems. Serious and persistent offenders, and those who dispute guilt, should go to a juvenile court dealing solely with criminal matters which would have a range of sanctions available to it including a custodial order which would be determinate and would attract remission. This new order would replace the present indeterminate training school order. We propose that the custodial unit should be managed by an independent management committee which will also be responsible for the management of the Probation Service. The Probation Service will have a central role in dealing with juvenile offenders.

9.7 Throughout our Report we refer to the contribution of the voluntary sector which has been of vital importance in the historical development of services and will continue to be so in the future. We are anxious that statutory bodies should recognise the importance of a strong voluntary sector and should take active steps to secure the participation and active involvement of voluntary and community bodies in the work of caring for children.

9.8 The standards of children are the standards of the wider society. How children grow up is affected by the social and economic environment and by the opportunity or otherwise of fulfilment. More than anything the behaviour of children is determined by the behaviour of adults—what they do and what they are seen to tolerate. There is a basic dishonesty in a society which demands from children higher standards of behaviour than adults have been prepared to tolerate for themselves.

9.9 We now set out a detailed list of our recommendations.

Recommendations

RECOMMENDATIONS—*cont'd*

19. The statutory bias in favour of boarding out should be removed   4.32

20. There should be a statutory delay on the removal of children from care, or from a foster home, as provided for in section 56 of the Children Act 1975   .   .   .   .   4.34

21. Custodianship orders in relation to fostering should not be introduced in Northern Ireland at present 4.35

22. There should be more hostel accommodation for adolescents   4.38

23. There should be specialist provision for young people with severe behavioural problems 4.38

24. There is a need to make adequate and appropriate provision for the education of children in residential care   .   .   4.39

25. Residential care staff should be encouraged to undertake appropriate training 4.42

26. A "visitor", on the lines of section 24 of the Children and Young Persons Act 1969, should be appointed for all children in care irrespective of age 4.43

27. The law relating to abuse should be re-drafted to encompass verbal and psychological abuse 4.46

28. The term "in need of care, protection, or control" as used in section 93 of the 1968 Act should be redefined   .   .   .   4.47

29. Children placed with a view to adoption should be subject to provisions of adoption law 4.49

30. The Department of Health and Social Services and the Department of Education should jointly, and in conjunction with the relevant agencies, examine the protective provisions of Part 1 of the 1968 Act 4.51

31. The Department of Health and Social Services and the Department of Education should jointly examine current legislation in Part III of the 1968 Act relating to the employment of children 4.53

Chapter 5—Welfare and Justice

32. There should be no change in the age of criminal responsibility   5.37

Chapter 6—Control of Delinquent Behaviour

33. There should be an extension of police cautioning.   .   .   6.2

34. Categories of offences to be regarded as minor and suitable for caution should be defined 6.6

35. Children charged with criminal offences should continue to be dealt with by a juvenile court 6.13

36. The Probation Service should be the main agency providing reports for the juvenile court 6.19

37. The juvenile court for criminal cases should retain the power to impose absolute or conditional discharge, binding-over, fine and the award of compensation 6.22

38. The existing provisions of section 73 of the 1968 Act relating to very serious crimes should be retained 6.29

39. There should be a single custodial order which would be determinate and which would attract remission . . . 6.29

40. There should be a single secure custodial unit for juvenile offenders 6.31

41. The juvenile court should consist of a full-time legally qualified chairman accompanied by two members drawn from a panel of lay people 6.38

42. Lay members of the juvenile court for criminal cases should be given the opportunity to become familiar with legal concepts and powers available to the court before full membership to the panel is ratified 6.39

43. There should be specialist magistrates dealing exclusively with all juvenile cases 6.42

Chapter 7—The Probation Service

44. The Probation Service should remain a separate service specialising in dealing with offenders and serving the criminal courts 7.4

45. The Probation Service should be administered by a Committee drawn from a wide spectrum of the community in Northern Ireland 7.5

46. A written code of practice should be drawn up by the Probation Service 7.6

47. The Probation Committee should have responsibility for the management of the custodial establishment 7.7

Chapter 8—Planning and Resources

48. In order that the voluntary sector should be able to make its views known on the future provision of services and facilities for children, a Standing Sub-Committee of the Central Personal Social Services Advisory Committee should be set up 8.4

APPENDIX

RESPONDENTS TO CONSULTATIVE DOCUMENT

Association of Boys' Clubs
Association of Community Home Schools
Association of Directors of Social Services*
Association of District Committees for the Health & Personal Social Services
Association of Nurse Administrators
Attendance Centre, Belfast

Barcroft, J. Esq., Consultant Child Psychiatrist
Belfast Central Mission
Borstal Visiting Committee*
British Association for Early Childhood Education
British Association of Social Workers*
British Psychological Society*

Catholic Child Welfare Group*
Central Council for Education & Training in Social Work
Central Council of Probation & After-Care Committees
Central Nursing & Midwifery Advisory Committee
Central Personal Social Services Advisory Committee*
Central Services Agency
Clark, Mrs Mary*
Conference of Chief Probation Officers
Council on Alcohol Related Problems*

Director of Public Prosecutions
Dr Barnardo's*

East Belfast Community Council
Eastern Health & Social Services Board*

Ferris, J. Esq., Educational Psychologist

Glendhu Children's Hostel Incorporated*

Home Office
Howard League for Penal Reform

Incorporated Law Society of Northern Ireland

Legal Action Group
Lisnevin Training School

McGregor, W. R. Esq., Reporter, Strathclyde Regional Council
Magilligan Prison Board of Visitors
Maxwell, P. Esq., RM*
Medico-Legal Society
Methodist Church in Ireland

National Association of Chief Education Welfare Officers
National Association for Care & Resettlement of Offenders
National Association of Probation Officers*
National Children's Bureau
National Consultative Group of Regional Chairmen of Children's Panels

National Society for the Prevention of Cruelty to Children
New University of Ulster
Northern Health & Social Services Board*
Northern Ireland Association of Boys' Clubs
Northern Ireland Association for Care & Resettlement of Offenders
Northern Ireland Association of Resident Magistrates*
Northern Ireland Council of Social Services*
Northern Ireland Juvenile Courts Association*
Northern Ireland Probation & After-Care Service*
Northern Ireland Public Service Alliance*

Prison Governors
Probation Projects Committee

Queen's University Belfast

Rathgael & Whiteabbey Schools Management Board*
Residential Care Association
Rogers, Professor Sinclair
Royal College of Midwives
Royal College of Nursing
Royal Ulster Constabulary

Scottish Association of Children's Panels
Scottish Education Department
Sisters of Nazareth
Southern Education & Library Board
Southern Health & Social Services Board*

Thompson, J. Daniel Esq.
Thompson, Mrs Joan
Todd, Brian Esq.
Training Schools Principals*

Webb, Mrs Rosemary, JP
Western Health & Social Services Board*
Wilson, J. Esq., Education Psychologist

Youth Committee for Northern Ireland

*Also gave oral evidence.

Printed in Northern Ireland for Her Majesty's Stationery Office
by Nelson & Knox (NI) Ltd Belfast   Dd 621732 K24 11/79 Gp 148

HER MAJESTY'S STATIONERY OFFICE

Government Bookshops
80 Chichester Street, Belfast BT1 4JY
49 High Holborn, London WC1V 6HB
13a Castle Street, Edinburgh EH2 3AR
41 The Hayes, Cardiff CF1 1JW
Brazennose Street, Manchester M60 8AS
Southey House, Wine Street, Bristol BS1 2BQ
258 Broad Street, Birmingham B1 2HE

Government publications are also available
through booksellers

ISBN 0 337 07200 0